FAST
Grade 7 Math Practice

GET DIGITAL ACCESS TO

 2 FAST Practice Tests

 Personalized Study Plans

REGISTER NOW

Link

QR Code

Visit the link below for online registration

lumoslearning.com/a/tedbooks

Access Code: FASTG7M-28160-P

Florida Assessment of Student Thinking (FAST) Test Prep: 7th Grade Math Practice Workbook and Full-length Online Assessments: FAST Study Guide

Contributing Editor - Aaron Spencer
Contributing Editor - Nikki McGee
Executive Producer - Mukunda Krishnaswamy
Program Director - Anirudh Agarwal
Designer and Illustrator - Sowmya R.

ISBN 13: 978-1949855951

Printed in the United States of America

FOR SCHOOL EDITION AND PERMISSIONS, CONTACT US

LUMOS INFORMATION SERVICES, LLC

 PO Box 1575, Piscataway, NJ 08855-1575
 www.LumosLearning.com

 Email: support@lumoslearning.com
 Tel: (732) 384-0146
Fax: (866) 283-6471

INTRODUCTION

This book is specifically designed to improve student achievement on the Florida Assessment of Student Thinking (FAST). Students perform at their best on standardized tests when they feel comfortable with the test content as well as the test format. Lumos online practice tests are meticulously designed to mirror the state assessment. They adhere to the guidelines provided by the state for the number of sessions and questions, standards, difficulty level, question types, test duration and more.

Based on our decade of experience developing practice resources for standardized tests, we've created a dynamic system, the Lumos Smart Test Prep Methodology. It provides students with realistic assessment rehearsal and an efficient pathway to overcoming each proficiency gap.

Use the Lumos Smart Test Prep Methodology to achieve a high score on the FAST.

Lumos Smart Test Prep Methodology

1 The student takes the first online diagnostic test, which assesses proficiency levels in various standards.

2 StepUp generates a personalized online study plan based on the student's performance.

3 The student completes targeted practice in the printed workbook and marks it as complete in the online study plan.

4 The student then attempts the second online practice test.

5 StepUp generates a second individualized online study plan.

6 Additional activities are planned to help the student gain comprehensive mastery for success on the FAST.

Table of Contents

Chapter 1
Number Sense and Operations

Lesson 1: Applying Laws of Exponents

1. **Simplify the expression: $3^4 \div 3^2$**

   $81 \div 9 = 9$

   Ⓐ 9
   Ⓑ 27
   Ⓒ 81
   Ⓓ 243

2. **Evaluate the value of $2^3 \times 2^5$**

   $8 \times 32 = 256$

   Ⓐ 16
   Ⓑ 32
   Ⓒ 128
   Ⓓ 256

3. **Which of the following expressions is equivalent to $(2^4)^3$?**

   Ⓐ 2^{12}
   Ⓑ 2^7
   Ⓒ 2^1
   Ⓓ 2^0

4. **Simplify the expression: $(5^2)^3 \times (5^3)^2$**

   $5^6 \times 5^6 = 5^{12}$

   Ⓐ 5^6
   Ⓑ 5^{12}
   Ⓒ 5^{15}
   Ⓓ 5^{30}

5. **Which of the following expressions is equivalent to $(\frac{2}{3})^5 \times (\frac{2}{3})^2$?**

   Ⓐ $(\frac{2}{3})^3$

   Ⓑ $(\frac{2}{3})^7$

   Ⓒ $(\frac{2}{3})^{10}$

   Ⓓ $(\frac{2}{3})^{35}$

6. **Simplify the expression: $(3^2)^3$**

   Ⓐ 6
   Ⓑ 27
   Ⓒ 81
   Ⓓ 729

7. **Evaluate the value of 4^0.**

   Ⓐ 0
   Ⓑ 1
   Ⓒ 4
   Ⓓ Undefined

8. **Simplify the expression: $(5^3)^2 \div 5^5$**

   Ⓐ $\dfrac{1}{5}$

   $5^6 \div 5^5$

   Ⓑ $\dfrac{1}{25}$

   Ⓒ 5
   Ⓓ 25

9. **Evaluate the value of $(\dfrac{1}{2})^4$.**

   Ⓐ $\dfrac{1}{2}$

   Ⓑ $\dfrac{1}{8}$

   Ⓒ $\dfrac{1}{16}$

   Ⓓ 8

10. **Simplify the expression: $(4^3 \times 4^2)^2$**

   Ⓐ $(\dfrac{1}{4})^5$

   Ⓑ 5
   Ⓒ 5
   Ⓓ 25

CHAPTER 1 → Lesson 2: Solving Multi-Step Problems

1. Bob, the plumber, charges $\frac{1}{4}$ the cost of materials as his labor fee. If his current job has a material cost of $130, how much will Bob charge his client (including his labor fee)?

    Ⓐ $162.50
    Ⓑ $32.50
    Ⓒ $130.25
    Ⓓ None of the above

2. A box has a length of 6x inches. The width equals one third the length, and the height equals half the length. If the volume equals 972 cubic inches, what does x equal?

    Ⓐ 5
    Ⓑ 2
    Ⓒ 3
    Ⓓ 4

3. Taylor is trimming the shrubbery along three sides of his backyard. The backyard is rectangular in shape. The length of the backyard is twice its width and the total perimeter is 180 feet.

    The shrubbery that Taylor needs to trim is along three sides of the rectangular backyard (along the two lengths and one width). Find the total length of the shrubbery that he needs to trim.

    Ⓐ 180 ft
    Ⓑ 120 ft
    Ⓒ 90 ft
    Ⓓ 150 ft

4. Jim is 4 years older than his brother Bob. In two years, Jim will be twice Bob's age. How old are they now?

    Ⓐ Bob is 6 and Jim is 10.
    Ⓑ Bob is 4 and Jim is 8.
    Ⓒ Bob is 0 and Jim is 4.
    Ⓓ Bob is 2 and Jim is 6.

5. In a certain classroom, the ratio of boys to girls is 2 to 1. If there are 39 students in the classroom, how many are boys?

   Ⓐ 18
   Ⓑ 22
   Ⓒ 26
   Ⓓ 30

6. John put three gallons of gasoline into his truck. The gasoline level was at 10% before he added the gasoline. If the truck has a 12 gallon tank, how much more gasoline can fit in the tank?

   Ⓐ 7.8 gallons
   Ⓑ 6.7 gallons
   Ⓒ 8.9 gallons
   Ⓓ 10.8 gallons

7. Melanie has $35.00 in her savings account and does cleaning in a neighbor's house for $15.00 per week. Sue has no money saved, but is mowing lawns at $20.00 each. If Sue mows 1 lawn per week, how long will it take her to catch up with Melanie?

   Ⓐ 5 weeks
   Ⓑ 6 weeks
   Ⓒ 7 weeks
   Ⓓ 8 weeks

8. Sissy is baking cookies for her class party. She plans to bake 128 cookies. Her recipe makes 6 dozen cookies. If her recipe calls for 3 1/2 c flour, how much flour will she need to make 128 cookies (round to the nearest half cup)?

   Ⓐ $5\frac{1}{2}$ c
   Ⓑ 4 c
   Ⓒ $4\frac{1}{2}$ c
   Ⓓ 6 c

9. Jenn went to the farmer's market with $40.00. She bought a 10 lb bag of potatoes for $6.00, a pie for $8.00, 4 qt fresh blueberries for $4.00 per qt, and 5 lb of apples at $1.49 per lb. What percent of the $40.00 did she still have when she left?

   Ⓐ 93.625%
   Ⓑ 6.375%
   Ⓒ 25%
   Ⓓ .0595%

10. Nelly spent $\frac{7}{8}$ of his savings on furniture and the rest on a lawnmower. If the lawnmower cost him $250, how much did he spend on furniture?

Ⓐ $2000
Ⓑ $1750
Ⓒ $1500
Ⓓ $1000

11. What is the perimeter of a rectangle where the width is x and the length is x + 4? Select the correct expressions.

Note: There is more than one correct answer.

Ⓐ x + 8
Ⓑ (x + 4) + x
Ⓒ x + x + (x +4) + (x + 4)
Ⓓ 4x + 8
Ⓔ zx + 4

12. Lisa is buying wallpaper for her room. The wallpaper costs $3.50 per foot. The wallpaper company also charges a $5 delivery fee per order. Let f represent the number of feet of wallpaper needed. Write an expression to represent how much Lisa will spend.

$$3.50f + 5$$

13. Which expression is the product of two factors and is equivalent to 3x - 27. Circle the correct answer choice.

Ⓐ 3 (x - 9)
Ⓑ -3 (3x -9)
Ⓒ 8x (8x - 15)
Ⓓ 3x (9x8)

CHAPTER 1 → Lesson 3: Rational Numbers, Addition & Subtraction

1. **Evaluate: 25 + 2.005 - 7.253 - 2.977**

   Ⓐ -16.775
   Ⓑ 16.775
   Ⓒ 167.75
   Ⓓ 1.6775

2. **Add and/or subtract as indicated :** $-3\dfrac{4}{5} + 9\dfrac{7}{10} - 2\dfrac{11}{20} =$

   Ⓐ $3\dfrac{7}{20}$

   Ⓑ $4\dfrac{7}{10}$

   Ⓒ $4\dfrac{9}{20}$

   Ⓓ $3\dfrac{1}{20}$

3. **Linda and Carrie made a trip from their hometown to a city about 200 miles away to attend a friend's wedding. The following chart shows their distances, stops and times. What part of their total trip did they spend driving?**

3hr	driving
15 min	rest stop
1 1/2 hr	driving
1 hr	rest stop
20 min	driving

   Ⓐ $\dfrac{4}{5}$

   Ⓑ $\dfrac{2}{5}$

   Ⓒ $\dfrac{58}{73}$

   Ⓓ $\dfrac{99}{100}$

4. If $a = \dfrac{5}{6}$, $b = -\dfrac{2}{3}$ and $c = -1\dfrac{1}{3}$, find a - b - c.

Ⓐ $-1\dfrac{1}{6}$

Ⓑ $2\dfrac{5}{6}$

Ⓒ $-2\dfrac{1}{6}$

Ⓓ $-2\dfrac{5}{6}$

5. If Ralph ate half of his candy bar followed by half of the remainder followed by half of that remainder, what part was left?

Ⓐ $\dfrac{1}{4}$

Ⓑ $\dfrac{1}{8}$

Ⓒ $\dfrac{1}{6}$

Ⓓ $\dfrac{1}{3}$

6. Mary is making a birthday cake to surprise her mom. She needs $3\dfrac{1}{2}$ cups of flour but she only has $\dfrac{1}{3}$ cup. How much more flour does she need?

7. Ricky purchased shoes for $159.95 and then exchanged them at a buy 1, get 1 half-off sale. The shoes that he purchased on his return trip were $74.99 and $68.55. How much did he receive back from the store after his second transaction? Note: The half-price applies to the cheaper of the two pairs.

   Ⓐ $37.50
   Ⓑ $68.55
   Ⓒ $34.28
   Ⓓ $50.68

8. Simplify the following expression:

   $3.24 - 1.914 - 6.025 + 9.86 - 2.2 + 5\dfrac{1}{2} =$

   Ⓐ -8.461
   Ⓑ 8.461
   Ⓒ -11.259
   Ⓓ 11.259

9. John had $76.00. He gave Jim $42.45 and gave Todd $21.34. John will receive $14.50 later in the evening. How much money will John have later that night?

   Ⓐ $25.71
   Ⓑ $26.67
   Ⓒ $26.71
   Ⓓ $24.71

10. Jeri has had a savings account since she entered first grade. Each month of the first year she saved $1.00. Each month of the second year she saved $2.00. This pattern of adding one additional dollar each month for an entire year continued until she was saving $10.00 per month in the tenth year. How much does she have saved at the end of ten years?

    Ⓐ $660
    Ⓑ $648
    Ⓒ $636
    Ⓓ $624

11. Solve : $\dfrac{3}{7} + \left(-\dfrac{5}{7}\right)$ Write your answer in the box given below.

12. Which expressions equal $-\dfrac{3}{4}$? Select all the correct answers.

Ⓐ $\dfrac{1}{8} - \dfrac{7}{8}$

Ⓑ $\dfrac{7}{8} - \dfrac{1}{8}$

Ⓒ $-\dfrac{6}{4} + \dfrac{3}{4}$

Ⓓ $\dfrac{1}{4} + \dfrac{1}{8}$

13. Read the number sentences below and match it with the correct associated property.

	Associative Property of Addition	Inverse Property of Addition	Identity Property of Addition
$\dfrac{2}{5} + 0 = \dfrac{2}{5}$	○	○	○
$\dfrac{1}{4} + \left(\dfrac{2}{3} + \dfrac{7}{8}\right) = \left(\dfrac{1}{4} + \dfrac{2}{3}\right) + \dfrac{7}{8}$	○	○	○
$\dfrac{6}{7} + \left(-\dfrac{6}{7}\right) = 0$	○	○	○

CHAPTER 1 → Lesson 4: Rational Numbers, Multiplication and Division

1. **Fill in the blank to make a true equation.**

   (-9)*(___) = 36

   (A) - 4
   (B) 4
   (C) 6
   (D) - 6

2. **Solve for x.**

   x = (-2)(6)(-4)

   (A) x = 36
   (B) x = 0
   (C) x = 48
   (D) x = - 48

3. **Simplify the following complex fraction.**

   $$\frac{\frac{1}{2}}{\frac{2}{3}}$$

   (A) $\frac{4}{3}$

   (B) $\frac{1}{2}$

   (C) $\frac{3}{4}$

   (D) $\frac{4}{3}$

4. Which of the following represents the product of 0.53 * 11.6?

   Ⓐ   0.6148
   Ⓑ   6.148
   Ⓒ   61.48
   Ⓓ   614.8

5. Which of the following is NOT a rational number?

   Ⓐ $\dfrac{8}{15}$

   Ⓑ   20.6
   Ⓒ $\sqrt{3}$

   Ⓓ $\dfrac{9}{11}$

6. Which of the following numbers is divisible by 3?

   Ⓐ   459,732
   Ⓑ   129,682
   Ⓒ   1,999,000
   Ⓓ   5,684,722

7. Which of the following fractions is equivalent to 0.625?

   Ⓐ $\dfrac{7}{9}$

   Ⓑ $\dfrac{5}{8}$

   Ⓒ $\dfrac{2}{3}$

   Ⓓ $\dfrac{8}{9}$

8. Mary wanted to estimate how many sheets of paper she had left. She knew that each sheet was about 0.1 mm thick. Her pack measured 2 cm thick.

   Which is the best estimate of the number of sheets of paper in Mary's pack?

   Ⓐ 50
   Ⓑ 100
   Ⓒ 150
   Ⓓ 200

9. Which of the following is the multiplicative inverse of $\dfrac{-7}{9}$?

   Ⓐ $\dfrac{7}{9}$

   Ⓑ $\dfrac{-9}{7}$

   Ⓒ $\dfrac{9}{7}$

   Ⓓ 1

10. Determine how many steps are necessary in a stairway between two floors that are 10.5 feet apart if each step is 9 inches high.

    Ⓐ 11 steps
    Ⓑ 12 steps
    Ⓒ 13 steps
    Ⓓ 14 steps

11. Shade the figure given to represent $\dfrac{2}{10} + \dfrac{3}{10}$

12. Fill in the table with correct multiplication expression for each division expression or the correct division expression for each multiplication expression.

Division Expression	Multiplication Expression
$\dfrac{\frac{-1}{3}}{\frac{7}{8}}$	$\dfrac{-1}{3} \times \dfrac{8}{7}$
$\dfrac{\frac{4}{3}}{-5}$	
$\dfrac{\frac{-6}{8}}{9}$	$-6 \times \dfrac{9}{8}$
	$\dfrac{-7}{3} \times \dfrac{9}{4}$
$\dfrac{\frac{-6}{11}}{\frac{-4}{5}}$	

13. Which of the following products are positive? Select all the correct answer choices.

Ⓐ $-\dfrac{2}{3} \times \dfrac{3}{4}$

Ⓑ $\dfrac{4}{5} \times \left(-\dfrac{2}{5}\right) \times (-3)$

Ⓒ $\left(-\dfrac{1}{8}\right)\left(-\dfrac{7}{8}\right)(10)$

Ⓓ $3\dfrac{4}{7} \times -2\dfrac{1}{2}$

CHAPTER 1 → Lesson 5: Strategies for Adding and Subtracting Rational Numbers

1. **What property is illustrated in the equation?:**

$$7 + \frac{1}{2} = \frac{1}{2} + 7$$

  Ⓐ Commutative property of addition
  Ⓑ Associate property of addition
  Ⓒ Distributive property
  Ⓓ Identity property of addition

2. **Which is a valid use of properties to make the expression easier to calculate?**

  92 – 8 = ?

  Ⓐ 90 – 2 – 8
  Ⓑ 82 – (10 – 8)
  Ⓒ 82 + (10 – 8)
  Ⓓ (80 + 2) – 8

3. **Find the sum of the mixed numbers.**

$$4\frac{7}{8} + 7\frac{5}{8}$$

  Ⓐ $11\frac{5}{8}$

  Ⓑ $12\frac{1}{2}$

  Ⓒ $12\frac{7}{8}$

  Ⓓ $11\frac{1}{2}$

4. **Which is a correct use of the distributive property?**

  Ⓐ 3(4+2) = 3(4)+2
  Ⓑ 3(4+2) = (3 x 4) x (3 x 2)
  Ⓒ 3(4+2) = 3(4)+3(2)
  Ⓓ All of the above

5. **Name the property illustrated in the equation:**

    (5 + 8) + 2 = 5 + (8 + 2)

    Ⓐ Distributive property
    Ⓑ Associative property of addition
    Ⓒ Commutative property of addition
    Ⓓ Identity property of addition

6. **Which is a valid use of properties to make the expression easier to calculate?**

    7 − 2.45

    Ⓐ (6 − 2) + (1 − 0.45)
    Ⓑ (7 − 2) + 0.45
    Ⓒ 5 + 0.45
    Ⓓ 7 − (0.45 − 2)

7. **Write the improper fraction as a mixed number.**

    $$\frac{31}{3}$$

    Ⓐ $3\frac{1}{3}$

    Ⓑ $30\frac{1}{3}$

    Ⓒ $31\frac{1}{3}$

    Ⓓ $10\frac{1}{3}$

8. **Find the difference between $16\frac{3}{4}$ - $9\frac{7}{8}$**

    Ⓐ $7\frac{1}{8}$

    Ⓑ $6\frac{7}{8}$

    Ⓒ $7\frac{7}{8}$

    Ⓓ $6\frac{1}{8}$

9. **What property is illustrated in the equation?:**

   (5 + 3) + 0 = 5 + 3

   Ⓐ Identity property of addition
   Ⓑ Associative property of addition
   Ⓒ Commutative property of addition
   Ⓓ Distributive property

10. **Which is a valid use of properties to make the expression easier to calculate? Circle the correct answer choice.**

    $$\frac{20}{7} - 1\frac{3}{7} =$$

    Ⓐ $\frac{20}{7} - 1 + \frac{3}{7}$

    Ⓑ $\frac{13}{7} - 1 + \frac{3}{7}$

    Ⓒ $\left(\frac{13}{7} - \frac{3}{7}\right) + (1 - 1)$

    Ⓓ $\frac{20}{7} - \frac{1}{7} - \frac{3}{7}$

11. **Which of the pairs of numbers are 13.7 units apart on a number line? More than 1 answer may be correct. Mark all the correct answers.**

    Ⓐ - 26.3 and - 12.6
    Ⓑ - 26.3 and 12.6
    Ⓒ 26.3 and - 12.6
    Ⓓ - 3.2 and 10.5

12. **Write the correct absolute value expression or distance description into the blanks in the table.**

Distance between 4 and -1	$\lvert-1-4\rvert$	$\lvert4-(-1)\rvert$
Distance between -4 and -1		$\lvert-4-(-1)\rvert$
Distance between 4 and 1	$\lvert1-4\rvert$	
	$\lvert1-(-4)\rvert$	$\lvert-4-1\rvert$

CHAPTER 1 → Lesson 6: Strategies for Multiplying and Dividing Rational Numbers

1. **Which of these multiplication expressions is equivalent to the division expression below?**

$$-\frac{4}{23} \div \frac{7}{58}$$

Ⓐ $-\frac{23}{4} \times \frac{58}{7}$

Ⓑ $-\frac{4}{23} \times \frac{58}{7}$

Ⓒ $-\frac{23}{4} \times \frac{7}{58}$

Ⓓ $-\frac{4}{23} \times \frac{7}{58}$

2. **Which property is illustrated in the following statement?**
   (5)(4)(7) = (7)(5)(4)

   Ⓐ Triple multiplication property
   Ⓑ Distributive property
   Ⓒ Commutative property of multiplication
   Ⓓ Associative property of multiplication

3. **Find the quotient:** $4 \div \frac{1}{2}$

   Ⓐ 4
   Ⓑ 8
   Ⓒ 2
   Ⓓ 16

4. **Which of the following is a helpful and valid way to rewrite the expression for evaluation :**
   3(123)

   Ⓐ 3(100) + 3(20) + 3(3)
   Ⓑ 3(100) + 23
   Ⓒ 100 + 3(23)
   Ⓓ 300 + 3(20) + 3

5. Which multiplication expression are equivalent to $\dfrac{7}{8} \div \dfrac{1}{15}$?

  Ⓐ $\dfrac{7}{8}$ x 15

  Ⓑ $\dfrac{7}{8}$ x $\dfrac{1}{15}$

  Ⓒ $\dfrac{8}{7}$ ÷ $\dfrac{1}{15}$

  Ⓓ $\dfrac{8}{7}$ x $\dfrac{1}{15}$

6. Which property is illustrated in the following statement?

(2 · 3) · 6 = 2 · (3 · 6)

  Ⓐ   Associate property of multiplication
  Ⓑ   Commutative property of multiplication
  Ⓒ   Identity property of multiplication
  Ⓓ   Reflexive property

7. Find the product: $\dfrac{3}{2}$ ⋆ $\dfrac{7}{6}$

  Ⓐ $\dfrac{10}{12}$

  Ⓑ $\dfrac{21}{6}$

  Ⓒ $\dfrac{7}{4}$

  Ⓓ $\dfrac{10}{8}$

8. **Find the quotient:** $\dfrac{6}{5} \div \dfrac{3}{25}$

   Ⓐ $\dfrac{2}{5}$

   Ⓑ 2

   Ⓒ $\dfrac{5}{2}$

   Ⓓ 10

9. **Find the product:** $\left(2\dfrac{1}{3} \right)\left(3\dfrac{1}{2} \right)$

   Ⓐ $\dfrac{49}{6}$

   Ⓑ $6\dfrac{1}{6}$

   Ⓒ $\dfrac{6}{5}$

   Ⓓ $5\dfrac{2}{5}$

10. **Find the quotient:** $\left(5\dfrac{1}{4} \right) \div \left(1\dfrac{1}{2} \right)$

   Ⓐ $\dfrac{5}{8}$

   Ⓑ $\dfrac{7}{2}$

   Ⓒ 45

   Ⓓ 7

11. Fill in the table with the correct reciprocals.

$\dfrac{6}{4}$	$\dfrac{4}{6}$
	$\dfrac{-19}{6}$
$\dfrac{5}{-64}$	
	4

CHAPTER 1 → Lesson 7: Solving Real World Problems

1. **Andrew has $9.39 but needs $15.00 to make a purchase. How much more does he need?**

   Ⓐ $6.39
   Ⓑ $5.61
   Ⓒ $5.39
   Ⓓ $6.61

2. **Ben has to unload a truck filled with 25 bags of grain for his horses. Each bag weighs 50.75 pounds.**

   How many total pounds does he have to move?

   Ⓐ 12,687.50 pounds
   Ⓑ 1,268.75 pounds
   Ⓒ 126.875 pounds
   Ⓓ 1250 pounds

3. **A Chinese restaurant purchased 1528.80 pounds of rice. If they received 50 identical bags, how much rice was in each bag?**

   Ⓐ 30.576 pounds
   Ⓑ 305.76 pounds
   Ⓒ 3.0576 pounds
   Ⓓ None of the above.

4. **Leila stopped at the coffee shop on her way to work. She ordered 2 bagels, 3 yogurts, and 1 orange juice. Bagels were $0.69 each, yogurts were $1.49 each, and orange juice was $1.75. What was Leila's total bill?**

   Ⓐ $7.60
   Ⓑ $3.93
   Ⓒ $5.16
   Ⓓ $5.42

5. **Mickey bought pizza and sodas for himself and four of his friends. The pizza was $17.49, and 5 sodas were $1.19 each.**

   If the pizza is sliced into 10 equal slices and each person eats 2 slices and drinks one soda, what is the cost to each person?

   Ⓐ $2.94
   Ⓑ $4.13
   Ⓒ $3.50
   Ⓓ $4.69

6. Alan has to keep within a $15.00 budget. Tax is 6.5%. What is Alan's total if he buys 1 notebook, 1 pack of paper, 1 set of dividers, 2 pens and 5 pencils?

3-Ring Notebook	$5.69
Notebook Paper	$1.39
Dividers	$1.45
Pens	$1.19
Pencils	$0.50

Ⓐ $10.88
Ⓑ $14.28
Ⓒ $13.41
Ⓓ $15.00

7. Sammy is mowing the lawn. The lawn is 30 ft by 20 ft. Sammy cut a strip 5 ft by 10 ft and ran out of gas. How much more does he need to mow?

Ⓐ 250 sq ft
Ⓑ 550 sq ft
Ⓒ 50 sq ft
Ⓓ 600 sq ft

8. Dustin has leased 5 acres of land to raise produce for the farmers' market. He has already planted $\frac{5}{8}$ of the land.

How many more acres does he need to plant?

Ⓐ $3\frac{1}{8}$ acres
Ⓑ 4 acres
Ⓒ $1\frac{7}{8}$ acres
Ⓓ $\frac{3}{8}$ acres

9. Taylor bought a bag of marbles weighing 5.25 lb. Before he got to the car, the bag broke, spilling many marbles. To find out if he had recovered all of his marbles, he weighed the bag at home.

He found that his bag of marbles now weighed 4.98 lb. What was the weight of the lost marbles?

Ⓐ 0.27 lb
Ⓑ 2.7 lb
Ⓒ 0.173 lb
Ⓓ 1.73 lb

10. **Which of the following is a correct statement about the multiplication of two integers?**

   Ⓐ If the signs are both negative, multiply the numbers and give the answer a negative sign.
   Ⓑ If the signs are both negative, multiply the numbers and give the answer a positive sign.
   Ⓒ If the signs are unlike, multiply the numbers and give the answer a positive sign.
   Ⓓ If the signs are unlike, multiply the numbers and give the answer the sign of the larger absolute value.

11. **Robert has $\frac{4}{7}$ of a bucket of water. John has $\frac{2}{3}$ of a bucket of water. If Robert and John combine their buckets of water, how many buckets of water will they have? Write your answer in simplest form. Write your answer in the box given below.**

12. **Frank lives $\frac{1}{2}$ blocks east of Mary. Mary lives $\frac{3}{5}$ blocks east of school. How many blocks east of school does Frank live? There can be more than 1 correct answer. Select all the correct ones.**

   Ⓐ $1\frac{1}{10}$
   Ⓑ $\frac{11}{10}$
   Ⓒ $\frac{3}{5}$
   Ⓓ $\frac{4}{2}$
   Ⓔ $\frac{4}{7}$

13. **Solve each equation and mark if the answer is negative, positive or zero.**

	Negative	Zero	Positive
$-\frac{6}{7}-\left(-\frac{6}{7}\right)$	○	○	○
$-5-\frac{3}{5}$	○	○	○
$\frac{3}{4}-\frac{1}{5}$	○	○	○

End of Number Sense and Operations

Chapter 1
The Number Sense and Operations
Lesson 1: Applying Laws of Exponents

Question No.	Answer	Detailed Explanations
1	A	When dividing two exponential expressions with the same base, subtract the exponents. In this case, we have $3^4 \div 3^2$, which is equal to $3^{(4-2)} = 3^2 = 9$.
2	D	When multiplying two exponential expressions with the same base, add the exponents. In this case, we have $2^3 \times 2^5$, which is equal to $2^{(3+5)} = 2^8 = 256$.
3	A	When raising an exponential expression to another exponent, multiply the exponents. In this case, $(2^4)^3$ is equal to $2^{(4\times3)} = 2^{12}$.
4	D	First, simplify each exponent within the parentheses: $5^{(2\times3)} = 5^6$, and $5^{(3\times2)} = 5^6$. Then, when multiplying exponential expressions with the same base, add the exponents. Thus, $(5^2)^3 \times (5^3)^2 = 5^6 \times 5^6 = 5^{(6+6)} = 5^{12}$.
5	C	To multiply two exponential expressions with the same base, add the exponents. In this case, $(\frac{2}{3})^5 \times (\frac{2}{3})^2$ is equal to $(\frac{2}{3})^{(5+2)} = (\frac{2}{3})^7$. Thus, the expression is equivalent to $(\frac{2}{3})^7$.
6	D	To simplify an expression with exponentiation, multiply the exponents. In this case, $(3^2)^3$ simplifies to $3^{(2\times3)} = 3^6 = 729$.
7	B	Any non-zero number raised to the power of 0 is equal to 1. Therefore, $4^0 = 1$.
8	C	When dividing two exponential expressions with the same base, subtract the exponents. In this case, $(5^3)^2 \div 5^5$ simplifies to $5^{(3\times2 - 5)} = 5^{(6-5)} = 5^1 = 5$.
9	B	To evaluate a fractional base raised to a positive exponent, raise the numerator to the power and the denominator to the same power. In this case, $(\frac{1}{2})^4$ is equal to $\frac{1^4}{2^4} = \frac{1}{16}$.
10	C	$(4^3 \times 4^2)$ is equal to $(4^{(3+2)})^2 = (4^5)^2$ which gives 4^{10}.

Lesson 2: Solving Multi-Step Problems

Question No.	Answer	Detailed Explanations
1	A	In order to find out how much Bill should charge his client, divide 130 by 4, and then add the quotient to 130: (1) $130 \div 4 = 32.50$ (2) $130 + 32.50 = \$162.50$
2	C	First, write the expressions based on the language in the problem: length = 6x width = $(\frac{1}{3})(6x)$ height = $(\frac{1}{2})(6x)$ Next, solve for x based on the formula for volume, lwh. (1) $6x \times ((\frac{1}{3})(6x)) \times ((\frac{1}{2})(6x)) = 972$ (2) $6x \times 2x \times 3x = 972$ (3) $12x^2 \times 3x = 972$ (4) $36x^3 = 972$ (divide each side by 36) (5) $x^3 = 27$ (6) $x = 3$
3	D	Let x be the width of the rectangular backyard. Length = 2x. Perimeter of the backyard = $x + 2x + x + 2x = 180$ ft. $6x = 180$ ft. $x = \frac{180}{6} = 30$ ft. = width of the backyard. Length of the backyard = $2x = 60$ ft. Total length of the shrubbery Taylor needs to trim = width+length+length = $x + 2x + 2x = 150$ ft.
4	D	Now : Bob's age = x, Jim's age = x + 4 In 2 years : Bob's age = x + 2, Jim's age = x + 4 + 2 = x + 6 It is given that, in 2 years, Jim's age is twice Bob's age. Therefore, we have, $x + 6 = 2(x + 2)$ $x + 6 = 2x + 4$ $2 = x$ = Bob $6 = x + 4$ = Jim Bob is 2, and Jim is 6.
5	C	Let x = number of girls, 2x = number of boys, $x + 2x = 39$, $3x = 39$, $x = 13$, girls $2x = 26$ boys
6	A	First, set up the equation based on the language of the problem: (1) Amount of gas = 3 gallons (2) Gas level = 10% (3) Tank capacity = 12 gallons (4) x = Amount of gallons needed to fill tank (5) Equation = 12 - (12(0.10) + 3) = x Next, solve for x (6) $12 - (1.2 + 3) = x$ (7) $12 - 4.2 = x$ (8) 7.8 gallons
7	C	Let n = number of weeks of work for Sue to catch up with Melanie $35 + 15n = 20n$, $35 = 5n$, $7 = n$ 7 weeks is the correct answer.
8	D	6 dozen = 72 cookies $\frac{128}{72} = 1\frac{56}{72} = 1\frac{7}{9}$ recipes $1\frac{7}{9} \times 3\frac{1}{2} = 6.22$ cups 6 c is the correct answer.

Question No.	Answer	Detailed Explanations
9	B	She spent 4 x $4.00 = $16.00 for blueberries and 5 x $1.49 = $7.45 for apples and $6.00 for potatoes and $8.00 for a pie $37.45 Total $40.00 - $37.45 = $2.55 left $\frac{\$2.55}{\$40.00}$=.06375= 6.375% left
10	B	$\frac{8}{8} - \frac{7}{8} = \frac{1}{8}$ on lawnmower $(\frac{1}{8})$s = 250, s = 8(250), s = $2000, (total savings) $\frac{7}{8}$ (2000) = $\frac{14000}{8}$ = 1750. $1750 is the correct answer.
11	C and D	To calculate the perimeter, you must add all sides together. So, the correct answer is x + x + (x + 4) + (x + 4) which is option C. If you combine like terms you get 4x + 8 which is Option D. Hence, C and D are correct options.
12	3.50f+5	If the wallpaper is 3.50 for one foot, then it is 3.50 times f for f feet. You also need to add the $5 delivery fee.
13	A	Since the question asks for a product, you know it has to be two factors multiplied together. If you factor out the 3, you are left with x - 9. Therefore 3(x-9) is the product of two factors that equals 3x - 27.

Lesson 3: Rational Numbers, Addition & Subtraction

Question No.	Answer	Detailed Explanations
1	B	Remember: adding and subtracting rational numbers works just like integers. If you need to carry or borrow, the rules remain the same. 25 + 2.005 - 7.253 - 2.977 27.005 - 7.253 - 2.977 , 19.752 - 2.977 = 16.775
2	A	$-3\frac{4}{5} + 9\frac{7}{10} - 2\frac{11}{20} = -3\frac{16}{20} + 9\frac{14}{20} - 2\frac{11}{20}$ $-5\frac{27}{20} + 9\frac{14}{20} = -5\frac{27}{20} + 8\frac{34}{20}$, $3\frac{7}{20}$ is the correct answer.
3	C	They spent 6 hours and 5 min total on their trip. Of that time, 4 hours and 50 minutes were spent driving. $4\frac{5}{6}$ hrs driving out of 6 $\frac{1}{12}$ hours. Converting into improper fractions we get $(\frac{29}{6})$ out of $(\frac{73}{12})$. $(\frac{29}{6}) \times (\frac{12}{73}) = \frac{58}{73}$ hours spent driving
4	B	If $a = \frac{5}{6}$, $b = -\frac{2}{3}$ and $c = -1\frac{1}{3}$, find a - b - c. $\frac{5}{6} - (-\frac{2}{3}) - (-1$ $\frac{1}{3}) = \frac{5}{6} + \frac{4}{6} + 1\frac{2}{6} = 1\frac{11}{6} = 2\frac{5}{6}$. $2\frac{5}{6}$ is the correct answer.
5	B	Starting with a full candy bar, we take away $\frac{1}{2}$ leaving $\frac{1}{2}$. Then we take away $\frac{1}{2}$ of the remaining half leaving $\frac{1}{4}$ of the original candy bar. Then we take away half of the $\frac{1}{4}$ leaving $\frac{1}{8}$ of the original bar. $\frac{1}{8}$ is the correct answer.

Question No.	Answer	Detailed Explanations
6		Number of more cup of flour required by Mary for making birthday cake = Number of cup of flour needed to prepare cake - Number of cup of flour Mary already has $= 3\frac{1}{2} - \frac{1}{3} = \frac{7}{2} - \frac{1}{3} = \frac{(21-2)}{6} = \frac{19}{6} = 3\frac{1}{6}$ Mary require $3\frac{1}{6}$ cup more flour to prepare the birthday cake.
7	D	On his second trip to the store he paid $74.99 plus half of $68.55. $74.99 + $34.28 = $109.27 $159.95 - 109.27 = $50.68 $50.68 is the correct answer.
8	B	First, we will change 5 1/2 to 5.5. Then we have 3.24 - 1.914 - 6.025 +9.86 -2.2 + 5.5 = 8.461 8.461 is the correct answer.
9	C	To solve this problem, list all the monetary values, along with the proper operation, before evaluating it. For this problem, words like "give" mean to subtract, while "receives" means to add. (1) 76.00 - 42.45 - 21.34 + 14.50 = (2) 33.55 - 21.34 + 14.50 = (3) 12.21 + 14.50 = (4) 26.71 Therefore, John will have $26.71 later that night.
10	A	Year 1 - $12.00, Year 2 - $24.00. Year 3 - $36.00. Year 4 - $48.00. Year 5 - $60.00. Year 6 - $72.00. Year 7 - $84.00. Year 8 - $96.00. Year 9 - $108.00. Year 10 - $120.00 Adding the totals for each year, we get $660.00. $660.00 is the correct answer.
11	$-\frac{2}{7}$	Since the denominators are the same just add the numerators. 3 + -5 = -2
12	A and C	$-\frac{6}{4} + \frac{3}{4}$ add the numerators and you get -3. So the fraction is $-\frac{3}{4}$ $\frac{1}{8} - \frac{7}{8} = 1 - 7 = -6$ and $\frac{-6}{8}$ simplifies to $\frac{-3}{4}$

Question No.	Answer	Detailed Explanations

13

	Associative Property of Addition	Inverse Property of Addition	Identity Property of Addition
$\dfrac{2}{5} + 0 = \dfrac{2}{5}$	○	○	●
$\dfrac{1}{4} + \dfrac{2}{3} + \dfrac{7}{8} = \dfrac{1}{4} + \dfrac{2}{3} + \dfrac{7}{8}$	●	○	○
$\dfrac{6}{7} + -\dfrac{6}{7} = 0$	○	●	○

The associative property of addition means that you can move grouping symbols and it does not change the value of the expression. The inverse property of addition means that you can add a number and its inverse together and you will get 0. The identity property of addition states that if you add 0 to a number it will not change the value.

Lesson 4: Rational Numbers, Multiplication and Division

Question No.	Answer	Detailed Explanations
1	A	Remember that when we multiply like signs, either (- * -) or (+ * +), the result is positive, and when we multiply unlike signs, the result is negative. Since we are multiplying some number by - 9 and get +36, we know that the sign of the unknown quantity is also negative. Now, 4 * 9 = 36; so - 4 * - 9 = 36. - 4 is the correct answer.
2	C	x = (-2)(6)(-4) = 48. Option C is the correct answer.
3	C	In order to solve $\frac{1}{2} \div \frac{2}{3}$. Keep the first fraction, change the division symbol into a multiplication symbol, and flip the second fraction before solving the problem. (1) $\frac{1}{2} \div \frac{2}{3}$ = (2) $\frac{1}{2} \times \frac{3}{2}$ = (3) $\frac{1 \times 3}{2 \times 2}$ = (4) $\frac{3}{4}$. $\frac{3}{4}$ is the correct answer.
4	B	To arrive at the answer, multiply 53 by 116 (without considering decimal places). The answer got is 6148. there are 2 digits after decimal place in multiplicand (0.53) and 1 digit after decimal place in the multiplier (11.6). Hence, we need to place the decimal point after the 3rd digit (2+1) when counting from right. So, the answer will be 6.148
5	C	Rational numbers are numbers that can be written as p/q where p & q are integers and q is not 0. To remember this definition, associate rational with ratio. √3 is the correct answer.
6	A	If the sum of the digits is divisible by 3, then the number is divisible by 3. The sum of the digits of 459,732 is 30 which is divisible by 3. Therefore, 459,732 is divisible by 3. 459,732 is the correct answer.
7	B	0.625 = $\frac{625}{1000}$ Now divide top and bottom by 125 to reduce to lowest terms. $\frac{625}{1000}$ = $\frac{5}{8}$. $\frac{5}{8}$ is the correct answer.
8	D	1 cm =10 mm. Therefore 2 cm = 20 mm. The pack was 20 mm thick. We know that, each sheet is 0.1 mm thick. Hence, the number of sheets in the pack will be $\frac{20}{0.1}$=200. Hence, answer choice D is the correct option.

Question No.	Answer	Detailed Explanations
9	B	Multiplicative inverse is another name for reciprocal. When you multiply a number by its multiplicative inverse, you get 1. $(-\frac{7}{9}) \times (-\frac{9}{7}) = \frac{63}{63} = +1$. The multiplicative inverse of $(-\frac{7}{9})$ is $(-\frac{9}{7})$. $(-\frac{9}{7})$ is the correct answer.
10	D	Change feet to inches so you are working with the same units. 10.5 ft = 12(10.5) = 126 inches. Now, we must determine the number of 9 inch steps by dividing the total distance between floors, 126 inches, by the height of each step, 9 inches. $\frac{126}{9} = 14$ steps 14 is the correct answer.
11		$\frac{2}{10} + \frac{3}{10} = \frac{5}{10} = \frac{1}{2}$. Therefore you need to shade 5 out of 10 boxes in the figure which is half of the figure.

12

Division Expression	Multiplication Expression
$\dfrac{\frac{-1}{3}}{\frac{7}{8}}$	$\dfrac{-1}{3} \times \dfrac{8}{7}$
$\dfrac{\frac{4}{3}}{-5}$	$\dfrac{4}{3} \times \dfrac{-1}{5}$
$\dfrac{\frac{-6}{8}}{9}$	$-6 \times \dfrac{9}{8}$
$\dfrac{\frac{-7}{3}}{\frac{4}{9}}$	$\dfrac{-7}{3} \times \dfrac{9}{4}$
$\dfrac{\frac{-6}{11}}{\frac{-4}{5}}$	$\dfrac{-6}{11} \times \dfrac{-5}{4}$

To change the division expression to a multiplication expression, change the division symbol to a multiplication symbol and change the divisor to its reciprocal.

| 13 | B and C | B and C are positive products because they have an even number of negative factors. |

Lesson 5: Strategies for Adding and Subtracting Rational Numbers

Question No.	Answer	Detailed Explanations
1	A	The commutative property states that parts of an addition statement can be written in any order and the same sum will result.
2	C	The 92 can be written as 82 + 10, so that the 10 and 8 can first be subtracted, and then the result can be added to 82.
3	B	The whole number parts can be added together, and the fraction parts can be added together, resulting in 11 and $\frac{12}{8}$. The $\frac{12}{8}$ part is a full $\frac{8}{8}$, or 1, and an additional $\frac{4}{8}$, so that we have 12 and $\frac{4}{8}$, which simplifies to 12 and $\frac{1}{2}$.
4	C	The distributive property only applies when there is addition or subtraction inside the parentheses and a number outside the parentheses being multiplied to what is inside the parentheses. When you multiply a sum by a number, you can multiply each addend by that number separately and then add the products. It can be represented as follows: $a(b + c) = ab + ac$.
5	B	The associative property of addition states that different parts of an addition statement can be grouped together in any manner, and the same sum will still result.
6	A	The 7 can be written as 6 + 1, and the 2.45 can be written as (2 + 0.45). Subtract the 2 from the 6 and the 0.45 from the 1.
7	D	$\frac{31}{3}$ is the same as $\frac{30}{3} + \frac{1}{3}$. $\frac{30}{3} = 10$, so we have 10 and $\frac{1}{3}$.
8	B	Let the 16 be 15 + 1, and then subtract the $\frac{7}{8}$ from the 1, leaving only $\frac{1}{8}$. You now have $15 + \frac{1}{8} + \frac{6}{8} - 9$ (Note that $\frac{3}{4}$ is written as $\frac{6}{8}$). Subtract the 9 from the 15, and add the fractions to arrive at 6 and $\frac{7}{8}$. Alternate Method : $16\frac{3}{4} = \frac{67}{4} = \frac{134}{8}, 9\frac{7}{8} = \frac{79}{8}$ Therefore, $16\frac{3}{4} - 9\frac{7}{8} = \frac{134}{8} - \frac{79}{8} = \frac{134 - 79}{8} = \frac{55}{8} = 6\frac{7}{8}$.
9	A	The identity property of addition states that if you add 0 to a value, the sum is the same as the value itself.

Question No.	Answer	Detailed Explanations
10	C	Let $\frac{20}{7}$ be $\frac{13}{7} + \frac{7}{7}$. Subtract the $\frac{3}{7}$ from the $\frac{13}{7}$, and let the $\frac{7}{7}$ be written as 1 and subtracted with the existing 1.
11	A and D	A and D are correct answers. $-26.3-(-12.6) = 13.7$ and $-3.2 - 10.5 = -13.7$

12		
Distance between 4 and -1	$\lvert -1-4 \rvert$	$\lvert 4-(-1) \rvert$
Distance between -4 and -1	$\lvert -1-(-4) \rvert$	$\lvert -4-(-1) \rvert$
Distance between 4 and 1	$\lvert 1-4 \rvert$	$\lvert 4-1 \rvert$
Distance between -4 and 1	$\lvert 1-(-4) \rvert$	$\lvert -4-1 \rvert$

The distance between two numbers is the absolute value of the difference between two numbers. It does not matter which number you place first because you are taking the absolute value of the difference.

Lesson 6: Strategies for Multiplying and Dividing Rational Numbers

Question No.	Answer	Detailed Explanations
1	B	When we divide a fraction by another fraction, flip the second fraction (interchange numerator and denominator) and then multiply with the first. $(-\frac{4}{23})$ divided by $(\frac{7}{58}) = (-\frac{4}{23}) \times (\frac{58}{7})$.
2	C	The commutative property states that multiplication can be done in any order and the same product will result.
3	B	Dividing by a fraction is the same thing as multiplying by the reciprocal of that fraction. Multiply, then, by 2 rather than dividing by $\frac{1}{2}$: $4 \times 2 = 8$.
4	A	The 3 must be multiplied by all three place values. The same product will result if writing it out in individual terms.
5	A	To find an equivalent expression, change the division symbol to a multiplication symbol and rewrite the second number as a reciprocal. $(\frac{7}{8}) \times (\frac{15}{1}) = (\frac{7}{8}) \times 15$.
6	A	The associative property of multiplication states that multiplication can be grouped in any way and the same product will result.
7	C	Multiply the numerators together and the denominators together. This results in a value of $\frac{21}{12}$, which simplifies to $\frac{7}{4}$.
8	D	Instead of dividing by $\frac{3}{25}$, multiply by the reciprocal, $\frac{25}{3}$. The result is $\frac{150}{15}$, which simplifies to 10.
9	A	Convert both mixed numbers to improper fractions, and multiply them: $(\frac{7}{3})(\frac{7}{2}) = \frac{49}{6}$.
10	B	Convert both fractions to *rational* numbers $(\frac{21}{4}) \div (\frac{3}{2})$ and multiply by the reciprocal $(\frac{21}{4}) \cdot (\frac{2}{3})$ equals $\frac{42}{12}$. $\frac{42}{12}$ reduces to $\frac{7}{2}$.

Question No.	Answer	Detailed Explanations

11

$\dfrac{6}{4}$	$\dfrac{4}{6}$
$\dfrac{6}{-19}$	$\dfrac{-19}{6}$
$\dfrac{5}{-64}$	$\dfrac{-64}{5}$
$\dfrac{1}{4}$	4

The reciprocal of a fraction or quotient is created by flipping the numerator and denominator.

Lesson 7: Solving Real World Problems

Question No.	Answer	Detailed Explanations
1	B	$15.00 - $9.39 = $ 5.61 is the correct answer.
2	B	50.75 x 25 = 1268.75 pounds 1268.75 pounds. Option B is the correct answer.
3	A	1528.80 pounds ÷ 50 bags = 30.576 pounds in each bag. Option A is the correct answer.
4	A	2 bagels @ $0.69 each = 2 x $0.69 = $1.38 3 yogurts @ $1.49 each = 3 x $1.49 = $4.47 1 orange juice @ $1.75 = $1.75 Total bill = $7.60 $7.60 is the correct answer.
5	D	The pizza was divided equally so each person's cost for pizza is $17.49 ÷ 5 = $3.50. Soda was $1.19 each. Add to find the total cost for each person. $3.50 + $1.19 = $4.69. $4.69 is the correct answer.
6	B	1 notebook = $5.69 1 pack paper = $1.39 1 set dividers = $1.45 2 pens = 2 x $1.19 = $2.38 5 pencils = 5 x $0.50 = $2.50 Subtotal = $13.41 Tax = .065 x $13.41 = $0.87 Total = $14.28 The answer is $14.28.
7	B	The lawn is 30 ft x 20 ft = 600 sq ft. He mowed 5 ft x 10 ft = 50 sq ft 600 sq ft - 50 sq ft = 550 sq ft 550 sq ft is the correct answer.
8	C	$\frac{5}{8} \times 5 = \frac{25}{8} = 3\frac{1}{8}$ acres already planted. $5 - 3\frac{1}{8} = 4\frac{8}{8} - 3\frac{1}{8}$ $= 1\frac{7}{8}$ acres remaining to plant. $1\frac{7}{8}$ acres is the correct answer.
9	A	5.25 - 4.98 = 0.27 lb 0.27 lb is the correct answer.
10	B	When multiplying or dividing two integers, like signs will always give a positive, and unlike signs will always give a negative sign. If the signs are both negative, multiply the numbers and give the answer a positive sign, is the correct answer.
11	$1\frac{5}{21}$	$\frac{4}{7} = \frac{(4 \times 3)}{(7 \times 3)} = \frac{12}{21}$ $\frac{2}{3} = \frac{(2 \times 7)}{(3 \times 7)} = \frac{14}{21}$ Adding the two fractions, we get, $\frac{12}{21} + \frac{14}{21} = \frac{26}{21} = 1\frac{5}{21}$

Question No.	Answer	Detailed Explanations
12	A and B	A and B are correct options.

$$\frac{1}{2} = \frac{(1 \times 5)}{(2 \times 5)} = \frac{5}{10}$$

$$\frac{3}{5} = \frac{(3 \times 2)}{(5 \times 2)} = \frac{6}{10}$$

Adding the two fractions, we get $\frac{5}{10} + \frac{6}{10} = \frac{11}{10} = 1\frac{1}{10}$

13

	Negative	Zero	Positive
$-\frac{6}{7} - \left(-\frac{6}{7}\right)$	○	●	○
$-5 - \frac{3}{5}$	●	○	○
$\frac{3}{4} - \frac{1}{5}$	○	○	●

1. Sum of a number and its additive inverse (i.e. the number with opposite sign) is always zero.

2. Sum of two or more negative numbers will always result in a negative number. In this case we have -5 – 3/5 which can be written as a sum of two negative numbers as (-5) + (-3/5)

= (-5/1 x 5/5) + (-3/5)

=-25/5 + (-3/5)

=-28/5

= -5 3/5

3. ¾ -1/5 = ¾ x 5/5 – 1/5 x 4/4 = 15/20 – 4/20 = 11/20

Chapter 2: Algebraic Reasoning

Lesson 1: Applying Properties to Rational Expressions

1. Ruby is two years younger than her brother. If Ruby's brother's age is A, which of the following expressions correctly represents Ruby's age?

    Ⓐ A - 2
    Ⓑ A + 2
    Ⓒ 2A
    Ⓓ 2 - A

2. Find the difference: 8n - (3n - 6) =

    Ⓐ -n
    Ⓑ 5n - 6
    Ⓒ 5n + 6
    Ⓓ 8n - 6

3. Find the sum:

    6t + (3t - 5) =

    Ⓐ 9t - 5
    Ⓑ 9t + 5
    Ⓒ 3t - 5
    Ⓓ 6t - 5

4. Combine like terms and factor the following expression.

    7x - 14x + 21x - 2

    Ⓐ 15x - 2
    Ⓑ 2(7x - 1)
    Ⓒ 42x - 2
    Ⓓ 21(x - 1)

5. Which of the following expressions is equivalent to:

    3(x + 4) - 2

    Ⓐ 3x + 10
    Ⓑ 3x + 14
    Ⓒ 3x + 4
    Ⓓ 3x + 5

6. **Simplify the following expression:**

$$\left(\frac{1}{2}\right)x + \left(\frac{3}{2}\right)x$$

Ⓐ 2x

Ⓑ $\left(\dfrac{5}{2}\right)$ x

Ⓒ - x

Ⓓ $\dfrac{x}{2}$

7. **Simplify the following expression:**

0.25x + 3 - 0.5x + 2

Ⓐ -0.25x + 5
Ⓑ 0.75x + 5
Ⓒ -0.25x + 1
Ⓓ 5.75x

8. **Which of the following statements correctly describes this expression?**

2x + 4

Ⓐ Four times a number plus two
Ⓑ Two more than four times a number
Ⓒ Four more than twice a number
Ⓓ Twice a number less four

9. **Which of the following statements correctly describes the following expression?**

$$\frac{2x - 3}{2}$$

Ⓐ Half of three less than twice a number
Ⓑ Half of twice a number
Ⓒ Half of three less than a number
Ⓓ Three less than twice a number

10. Which of the following expressions is not equivalent to:

$$\left(\frac{1}{2}\right)(2x + 4) - 3$$

   Ⓐ (x + 2) - 3

   Ⓑ $\left(\frac{1}{2}\right)(2x + 4) - 3$

   Ⓒ x - 1

   Ⓓ x + 1

11. Which property is demonstrated in the following expression?

12(3x - 9) = 36x - 108

   Ⓐ Associative property

   Ⓑ Distributive property

   Ⓒ Identity property of addition

   Ⓓ Zero property of multiplication

12. Rhonda is purchasing fencing to go around a rectangular lot which is 4x + 9 ft long and 3x - 5 ft wide. Which expression represents the amount of fencing she must buy?

   Ⓐ 7x + 4

   Ⓑ 7x - 4

   Ⓒ 14x + 28

   Ⓓ 14x + 8

13. Rebekah is preparing for a swim meet. She is trying to swim 1 mile in 7 minutes. If the pool is 5x + 3 ft long, which expression represents how many laps she needs to swim in 7 minutes?

Assume 1 length of the pool is 1 lap. (1mile = 5280 feet.)

   Ⓐ 7(5x + 3)

   Ⓑ 5x + 3

   Ⓒ $\dfrac{5280}{5x + 3}$

   Ⓓ 5280(5x + 3)

14. **Simplify.**

    5x + 10y + 0(z) =

    Ⓐ 0
    Ⓑ 5x + 10y
    Ⓒ 15xy
    Ⓓ 5x

15. **Which property is demonstrated below?**

    2 + (8 + 3) = (2 + 8) + 3

    Ⓐ Additive Identity Property
    Ⓑ Multiplicative Identity Property
    Ⓒ Distributive Property
    Ⓓ Associative Property of Addition

16. **Use the Distributive Property to expand the expression 6(5x – 3). Write your answer in the box given below.**

17. **Which expressions are equal to 60x - 24? There is more than one correct answer. Select all the correct expressions.**

    Ⓐ 10(6x - 2)
    Ⓑ 4(10x - 6)
    Ⓒ 5(12x - 5)
    Ⓓ 6(10x - 4)
    Ⓔ -6(-10x + 4)
    Ⓕ 4(15x - 6)

18. **A bookstore is advertising $2 off the price of each book. You decide to buy 8 books. Let p represent the price of each book. Use the expression 8(p – 2) to find out how much you would spend if the regular price of each book is $13.**

    Write your answer in the box given below.

CHAPTER 2 → Lesson 2: Interpreting the Meanings of Expressions

1. **Which of the following expressions represents "5% of a number"?**

   Ⓐ 5n
   Ⓑ 0.5n
   Ⓒ 0.05n
   Ⓓ 500n

2. **Jill is shopping at a department store that is having a sale this week. The store has advertised 15% off certain off-season merchandise. Jill calculates the sales price by multiplying the regular price by 15% and then subtracting that amount from the regular price: SP = RP - 0.15(RP), where SP = Sales Price and RP = Regular Price. Find a simpler way for Jill to calculate the sales price as she shops.**

   Ⓐ SP = 0.15 RP
   Ⓑ SP = 1.15 RP
   Ⓒ SP = 0.85 RP
   Ⓓ SP = 1.85 RP

3. **Rewrite the following expression for the perimeter of a rectangle.**

   P = l + w + l + w, where P = perimeter, l = length, and w = width.

   Ⓐ P = l + 2w
   Ⓑ P = l + w
   Ⓒ P = 2(l) + w
   Ⓓ P = 2(l + w)

4. **If an item costs a store x dollars to buy and can be sold at y dollars, what percentage of the sale price is profit?**

   percentage of the sale price = [profit ÷ sale price] 100

   Which of the following rewrites this expression and includes the given information?

   Ⓐ $\dfrac{y - x}{100y}$

   Ⓑ $\dfrac{100(y - x)}{y}$

   Ⓒ $\dfrac{x - y}{100y}$

   Ⓓ $\dfrac{100(x - y)}{y}$

5. To find the average of five consecutive integers beginning with x, we add the integers and divide by 5.

Expressed in mathematical symbols, we have (x + x + 1+ x + 2 + x + 3 + x + 4) / 5 = Average (a)

Rewrite this expression another way.

Ⓐ x + 4
Ⓑ x + 3
Ⓒ x + 2
Ⓓ None of the above.

6 The bank will charge a 10% overdraft fee for any money withdrawn over the amount available in an account. If Jared has d dollars in the bank and he withdraws (d + 5) dollars, the bank charges 0.10{(d + 5) - d}. Find a simpler way of rewriting his overdraft fee.

Ⓐ 0.10(d + 5)
Ⓑ $0.50
Ⓒ $5.00
Ⓓ $2.50

7. Bob has been logging the days that the temperature rises over 100° in Orlando. He found that on 18 of the past 30 days the temperature rose above 100°.

Using this information, he made the following prediction of the number of days out of the next n days that the temperature would NOT rise above 100°:

$P = \left| \dfrac{30 - 18}{30} \right|$ n days. Find another way to write this expression.

Ⓐ $\left(\dfrac{2}{5}\right)$ n days

Ⓑ $\left(\dfrac{3}{5}\right)$ n days

Ⓒ $\left(\dfrac{4}{5}\right)$ n days

Ⓓ n days

8. If Roni runs for 20 minutes, walks for 10 and then runs for 15 while covering a total distance of m miles, her rate would be represented by:
r = m /{(20 + 10 +15) / 60} mph. Which of the following is a simpler representation of this formula?

Ⓐ r =(m/45) mph
Ⓑ r = (4/3m) mph
Ⓒ r = (45m/60) mph
Ⓓ r = (4m/3) mph

9. Hannah is taking piano lessons. Her mother has told her that each week she takes lessons, she has to practice $\frac{1}{2}$ hour more than she did the week before. Hannah created the following table. Write a simple expression to find the time she will practice in week 5n?

Piano Practice Time Sheet

Week	Time
1	1
2	1 1/2
n	1 + (1/2) (n-1)

Ⓐ $\frac{1 + 5n}{2}$ hr.

Ⓑ $\frac{5n}{2}$ hr.

Ⓒ $\frac{5n - 1}{2}$ hr.

Ⓓ $1 + \frac{5n}{2}$ hr.

10. The diameter of the Sun at the equator is 1,400,000 km. d = 1,400,000 km

Which of the following is another way to write this expression?

Ⓐ d = 1.4 x 10^6 km
Ⓑ d = 1.4 x 10^{-6} km
Ⓒ d = 14 x 10^6 km
Ⓓ d = 14 x 10^{-6} km

11. Which is another way of writing the following mathematical expression?

(6x - 15y - 2x + y) / -4(x - y)

Ⓐ $\frac{2x - 7y}{-2x - 2y}$

Ⓑ $\frac{2x - 7y}{-2}$

Ⓒ 5/2

Ⓓ $\frac{2x - 7y}{-2(x-y)}$

12. Which of the following expressions represents "a 24% increase"?

   Ⓐ n + 0.24
   Ⓑ n + 0.24n
   Ⓒ n + 24
   Ⓓ n + 24n

13. Ted is monitoring the scores of his two favorite football teams. He has a bet that Team A will finish with 19 points ahead of Team B.
He has made the following statement: Team A score -19 = Team B score. Which of the following is another way of making the same statement?

   Ⓐ Team B Score - 19 points = Team A Score
   Ⓑ Team B Score / Team A Score = 19 points
   Ⓒ Team A Score + Team B Score = 19 points
   Ⓓ Team A Score = Team B Score + 19 points

14. Linda bought 3 packages of red/white/blue ribbon for a rally. Each package held 3 rolls at 50 yd long and 3 rolls at 25 yd long, and each package cost $6.99.

Cost / yd = [3($6.99)] / 3[3(50) + 3(25)]

What is the cost/yd?

   Ⓐ $0.031/yd
   Ⓑ $0.31/yd
   Ⓒ $3.10/yd
   Ⓓ $2.10/yd

15. Jack went to the feed store to buy grain for his livestock. He bought fifty-five 50 lb bags.

Cost = $40/bag, but for every 10 bags, he got 1 free.

The following mathematical expression shows the cost/lb.

Cost/lb=$40(50)/[50(50) + 5(50)]

Which of the following is a simpler way of writing the above expression?

   Ⓐ Cost/lb = $50(50) / [40(55)]
   Ⓑ Cost/lb = $50(50) / [40(50)]
   Ⓒ Cost/lb = $40(55) / [50(50)]
   Ⓓ Cost/lb = $40(50) / [55(50)]

16. Sarah received a coupon for 15% off the total purchase price at a shoe store. Let p be the original price of the purchase. Use the expression p – 0.15p for the new price of the purchase. Write an equivalent expression by combining like terms.

17. Which of the expressions have like terms? There are more than 1 correct answer. Select all the correct answer choices

Ⓐ 4xy - 8y

Ⓑ -7x + 3x

Ⓒ h + 9.3h

Ⓓ 5t + 5

Ⓔ 12df - 3df

Ⓕ 8x - 2y

CHAPTER 2 → Lesson 3: Linear Inequality Word Problems

1. The annual salary for a certain position depends upon the years of experience of the applicant. The base salary is $50,000, and an additional $3,000 is added to that per year of experience, y, in the field. The company does not want to pay more than $70,000 for this position, though. Which of the following inequalities correctly expresses this scenario?

    (A) $53,000y \leq 70,000$
    (B) $3,000y \leq 50,000$
    (C) $50,000 + 3,000y \leq 70,000$
    (D) $3,000 + 50,000y \leq 70,000$

2. Huck has $225 in savings, and he is able to save an additional $45 per week from his work income. He wants to save enough money to have at least $500 in his savings. If w is the number of weeks, express this situation as an inequality.

    (A) $265w \geq 500$
    (B) $225 + 45w \geq 500$
    (C) $225 \leq 45w$
    (D) $225 + 45w \leq 500$

3. Lucy is charging her phone. It has a 20% charge right now and increases by an additional 2% charge every 3 minutes. She doesn't want to take it off the charger until it is at least 75% charged. If m is the number of minutes Lucy keeps her phone for charging, express this situation in an inequality.

    (A) $20 + \dfrac{2}{3} m \leq 75$

    (B) $20m + \dfrac{2}{3} m \leq 75$

    (C) $75 + \dfrac{2}{3} m \geq 20$

    (D) $20 + \dfrac{2}{3} m \geq 75$

4. Matt's final grade, G, in class depends on his last test score, t, according to the expression $G = 74 + 0.20t$. If he wants to have a final grade of at least 90.0, what is the minimum score he can make on the test?

    (A) 80
    (B) 74
    (C) 92
    (D) 86

5. Students can figure out their grade, G, on the test based upon how many questions they miss, n. The formula for their grade is G = 100 − 4n. If Tim wants to make at least an 83, what is the maximum number of questions he can miss?

Ⓐ 5 questions
Ⓑ 3 questions
Ⓒ 4 questions
Ⓓ 6 questions

6. The necessary thickness, T, of a steel panel in mm depends on the unsupported length, L, of the panel in feet according to the inequality T ≥ 3 + 0.2L. If the thickest panel available has a thickness of 12 mm, what is the maximum length it can span?

Ⓐ 75 ft
Ⓑ 45 ft
Ⓒ 60 ft
Ⓓ 54 ft

7. The pay that a salesperson receives each week is represented by the inequality P ≥ 300 + 25s, where s represents the number of units the salesperson sells. What is the significance of the number 300 in this inequality in this context?

Ⓐ The salesperson will never make more than $300 weekly.
Ⓑ The salesperson has never sold more than 300 units in a week.
Ⓒ The salesperson is guaranteed at least $300 even if he doesn't sell any units.
Ⓓ $300 is the price of a single unit.

8. The net calories gained or lost by a dieter depends on the hours exercised in a week according to the equation C = 750 − 200h. Based on his goals, Neil determines that the following inequality is necessary for him: h > 3.75. What is the significance of the value of this inequality?

Ⓐ Neil will lose at least 3.75 pounds per week if he meets this inequality.
Ⓑ Neil will lose weight each week if he meets this inequality.
Ⓒ Neil can eat only 375 calories on any given day.
Ⓓ If Neil meets this inequality, he will be able to eat as many calories as he likes.

9. A school always allows twice as many girls as boys to enroll in swimming classes each year. They also follow a certain inequality for the number of boys, B, and girls, G, in their admissions: B + G ≤ 300. What significance does this inequality have for the number of boys that can be admitted each year?

Ⓐ At least 200 boys must be admitted.
Ⓑ No more than 100 boys can be admitted.
Ⓒ The number of boys admitted must equal the number of girls.
Ⓓ No more than 150 boys can be admitted.

10. Isaac has to do at least 4 hours of chores each week. For each hour of television he watches, that minimum number of hours increases by 0.25. This week, the inequality for his hours of chores is h ≥ 5.5. What does this indicate about his television watching?

- Ⓐ He watched 6 hours of television this week.
- Ⓑ He watched 5.5 hours of television this week.
- Ⓒ He watched 22 hours of television this week.
- Ⓓ He watched no television this week.

11. The initial cost to rent a bike is $5. Each hour the bike is rented costs $2. Liz is going to rent a bike and can spend at most $17. Write and solve an inequality to find how long she can rent the bike.

12. Some friends put their money together to buy frozen treats from an ice cream truck. Two people got popsicles. Two people got ice cream cones. Each ice cream cone costs twice as much as popsicle. Two people ordered double scoops. Each double scoop cost three times as much as a popsicle. The total cost for their treats was less than $24.12. What are two possible prices for a popsicle? Write and solve the inequality.

- Ⓐ $2.03
- Ⓑ $2.02
- Ⓒ $2.01
- Ⓓ $2.00
- Ⓔ $1.95

13. A garden center sells 21 trays of red flowers, 12 trays of yellow flowers, and 16 trays of pink flowers every day. The gardener wants to know how many days, d, it will take to sell more than 200 trays of flowers. Which inequality models the situation.

Ⓐ 21d + 12d + 16d <200
Ⓑ 21d + 12d + 16d >200
Ⓒ 200 ≤ 21d + 16d + 12d
Ⓓ 200 ≥ 21d + 16d + 12d

CHAPTER 2 → Lesson 4: Modeling Using Equations or Inequalities

1. A 30 gallon overhead tank was slowly filled with water through a tap. The amount of water (W, in gallons) that is filled over a period of t hours can be found using W = 3.75(t). If the tap is opened at 7 AM and closed at 3 PM, how much water would be in the tank? Assume that the tank is empty before opening the tap.

   Ⓐ 18 gallons
   Ⓑ 20 gallons
   Ⓒ 24 gallons
   Ⓓ The tank is full

2. The ratio (by volume) of milk to water in a certain solution is 3 to 8. If the total volume of the solution is 187 cubic feet, what is the volume of water in the solution?

   Ⓐ 130 cubic feet
   Ⓑ 132 cubic feet
   Ⓒ 134 cubic feet
   Ⓓ 136 cubic feet

3. A box has a length of 12 inches and width of 10 inches. If the volume of the box is 960 cubic inches, what is its height?

   Ⓐ 6 inches
   Ⓑ 10 inches
   Ⓒ 12 inches
   Ⓓ 8 inches

4. Jan is planting tomato plants in her garden. Last year she planted 24 plants and harvested 12 bushels of tomatoes during the season. This year she has decided to only plant 18 plants. If the number of plants is directly proportional to the number of bushels of tomatoes harvested, how many bushels of tomatoes should she expect this year?

   Ⓐ 6
   Ⓑ 18
   Ⓒ 12
   Ⓓ 9

5. Melanie's age added to Roni's age is 27. Roni's age subtracted from Melanie's age is 3. Find their ages.

   Ⓐ 17, 10
   Ⓑ 16, 11
   Ⓒ 15, 12
   Ⓓ 14, 13

6. Tim wraps presents at a local gift shop. If it takes 2.5 meters of wrapping paper per present, how many can Tim wrap if he has 50 meters of wrapping paper?

Ⓐ 18
Ⓑ 20
Ⓒ 15
Ⓓ 17

7. Name the property demonstrated by the equation.

11 + (8 + 6) = (y + 8) + 6. Also, find the value of y?

Ⓐ 11, Commutative Property of Addition
Ⓑ 11, Associative Property of Addition
Ⓒ 11, Distributive Property
Ⓓ 11, Associative Property of Multiplication

8. In the linear equation p = 2c + 1, c represents the number of couples attending a certain event, and p represents the number of people at that event.

If there are 7 couples attending, how many people will be present?

Ⓐ 7 people
Ⓑ 14 people
Ⓒ 15 people
Ⓓ 16 people

9. The ratio (by volume) of salt to sugar in a certain mixture is 4 to 8. If the total volume of the mixture is 300 cubic feet, what is the volume of sugar in the mixture?

Ⓐ 200 cubic feet
Ⓑ 199 cubic feet
Ⓒ 201 cubic feet
Ⓓ 136 cubic feet

10. Which of the following sequences follows the rule $(8 + t^2) - 2t$ where t is equal to the number's position in the sequence?

Ⓐ 7, 8, 11, 16, 23, ...
Ⓑ 9, 12, 17, 24, 33 ...
Ⓒ 3, 4, 5, 6, 7, ...
Ⓓ 7, 10, 15, 22, 31, ...

11. Use the model to solve the equation. Circle the correct answer choice.

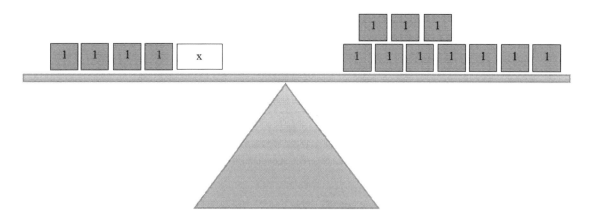

Ⓐ 6
Ⓑ 4
Ⓒ 1
Ⓓ 10

12. Which equation correctly represents the model and what is the solution?

Note: Select the answers that have the correct equation and solution. There is more than one correct answer.

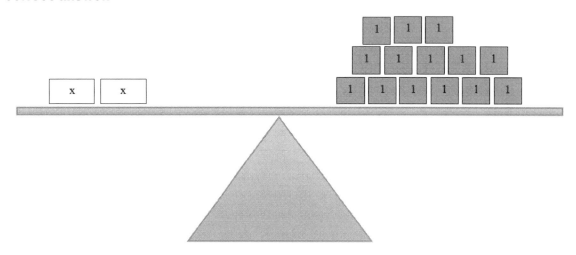

Ⓐ 2x = 14 and x = 7
Ⓑ x + 2 = 14 and x = 12
Ⓒ 2 + x = 14 and x = 12
Ⓓ x + x = 14 and x = 7
Ⓔ 2 = 14x and x = 0.5

CHAPTER 2 → Lesson 5: Applying Ratios and Percents

1. **What value of *x* will make these two expressions equivalent?**

   $$\frac{-3}{7} \text{ and } \frac{x}{21}$$

   Ⓐ x = -3
   Ⓑ x = 7
   Ⓒ x = 9
   Ⓓ x = -9

2. **If *p* varies proportionally to *s*, and *p* = 10 when *s* = 2, which of the following equations correctly models this relationship?**

   Ⓐ p = 5s
   Ⓑ p = 10s
   Ⓒ s = 10p
   Ⓓ 2s = 10p

3. **Solve for x, if $\frac{72}{108}$ and $\frac{x}{54}$ are equivalent.**

   Ⓐ x = 18
   Ⓑ x = 36
   Ⓒ x = 54
   Ⓓ x = 24

4. **At one particular store, the sale price, *s*, is always 75% of the displayed price, *d*. Which of the following equations correctly shows how to calculate *s* from *d*?**

   Ⓐ d = 75s
   Ⓑ s = 0.75d
   Ⓒ s = d - 0.75
   Ⓓ s = d + 75

5. **When *x* = 6, *y* = 4. If *y* is proportional to *x*, what is the value for *y* when *x* = 9?**

   Ⓐ   4

   Ⓑ $\frac{2}{3}$

   Ⓒ   3
   Ⓓ   6

6. Jim is shopping for a suit to wear to his friend's wedding. He finds the perfect one on sale at 30% off. If the original price was $250.00, what will the selling price be after the discount?

Ⓐ $75
Ⓑ $175
Ⓒ $200
Ⓓ $220

7. If Julie bought her prom dress on sale at 15% off and paid $110.49 before tax, find the original price of her dress.

Ⓐ $126.55
Ⓑ $129.99
Ⓒ $135.00
Ⓓ $139.99

8. A plot of land is listed for sale with the following measurements: 1300 ft x 982 ft. When the buyer measured the land, he found that it measured 1285 ft by 982 ft. What was the % of error of the area of the plot?

Ⓐ 1.47%
Ⓑ 14.73%
Ⓒ 1.15%
Ⓓ 11.7%

9. Pierre received a parking ticket whose cost is $22.00. Each month that he failed to make payment, fees of $7.00 were added. By the time he paid the ticket, his bill was $36.00. What was the ratio of fees to the cost of the ticket?

Ⓐ $\dfrac{36}{22}$

Ⓑ $\dfrac{22}{36}$

Ⓒ $\dfrac{7}{22}$

Ⓓ $\dfrac{7}{11}$

10. Sara owns a used furniture store. She bought a chest for $42 and sold it for $73.50. What percent did she mark up the chest?

Ⓐ 100%
Ⓑ 75%
Ⓒ 42%
Ⓓ 31.5%

11. What is 30% of 64? Enter your answer in the box given below.

12. Which of the expressions equals 60%? There can be more than 1 correct answer, select all the correct answers.

Ⓐ 48 of 100
Ⓑ 32.4 of 54
Ⓒ 3 of 5
Ⓓ 4 of 5
Ⓔ 32 of 53

13. Read each of the equation and match it to whether it is part, percent or whole.

	Part	Percent	Whole
What is 35% of 15?	☐	☐	☐
4% of what number is 46?	☐	☐	☐
y = .76 X 43	☐	☐	☐
14 = m X 56	☐	☐	☐

CHAPTER 2 → Lesson 6: Unit Rates

1. **A tennis match was delayed because of rain. The officials were not prepared for the delay. They covered the 25ft by 20ft court with 13ft by 10ft plastic covers. How many plastic covers were needed to cover the court from the rain?**

   Ⓐ 3 plastic covers
   Ⓑ 4 plastic covers
   Ⓒ 5 plastic covers
   Ⓓ 6 plastic covers

2. **John eats a bowl of cereal for 3 of his 4 meals each day. He finishes two gallons of milk in eight days. How much milk does John use for one bowl of cereal? (Assume he only uses the milk for his cereal.)**

   Ⓐ One-twelfth of a gallon of milk
   Ⓑ One cup of milk
   Ⓒ Two cups of milk
   Ⓓ One-sixth of a gallon of milk

3. **A recipe to make a cake calls for three-fourths of a cup of milk. Mary used this cake as the first layer of a wedding cake. The second layer was half the size of the first layer, and the third layer was half the size of the second layer. How much milk would be used for the entire wedding cake?**

   Ⓐ One and two-thirds cups of milk
   Ⓑ One and one-third cups of milk
   Ⓒ One and five-sixteenths cups of milk
   Ⓓ One cup of milk

4. **One third of a quart of paint covers one fourth of a basketball court. How much paint does it take to paint the entire basketball court?**

   Ⓐ one and one-third quarts
   Ⓑ one quart
   Ⓒ one and one-fourth quarts
   Ⓓ one and three-fourths quarts

5. **The total cost of 100 pencils purchased at a constant rate is $39.00. What is the unit price?**

    (A) $39.00
    (B) $3.90
    (C) $0.39
    (D) $0.039

6. **A construction worker was covering the bathroom wall with tiles. He covered three-fifths of the wall with 50 tiles. How many tiles will it take to cover the entire wall?**

    (A) 83 tiles
    (B) 83 and one-third tiles
    (C) 85 tiles
    (D) 83 and one-half tiles

7. **Jim ran four-fifths of a mile and dropped out of the 1600 meter race. His pace was 12 miles an hour until the point he dropped out of the race. How many minutes did he run?**

    (A) 4 minutes and 30 seconds
    (B) 4 minutes
    (C) 4 minutes and 20 seconds
    (D) 4 minutes and 10 seconds

8. **Ping played three-fourths of a football game. The game was three and a half hours long. How many hours did Ping play in this game?**

    (A) 2 hours 37 minutes
    (B) 2 hours 37 minutes and 30 seconds
    (C) 2 hours 37 minutes and 20 seconds
    (D) 2 hours 37 minutes and 10 seconds

9. **Bill is working out by running up and down the steps at the local stadium. He runs a different number of steps in random order.**

    Which of the following is his best time of steps per minute?

    (A) 25 steps in 5 minutes
    (B) 30 steps in 5.5 minutes
    (C) 20 steps in 4.5 minutes
    (D) 15 steps in 4 minutes

10. Doogle drove thirty and one-third miles toward his brother's house in one-third of an hour. About how long will the entire hundred mile trip take at this constant speed?

Ⓐ 1 hour
Ⓑ 1 hour and 6 minutes
Ⓒ 1 hour and 1 minutes
Ⓓ 1 hour and 3 minutes

11. A store is selling T-Shirts. Which is the best deal? Select all correct answers that apply.

Ⓐ 8 for $26
Ⓑ 5 for $30
Ⓒ 4 for $15
Ⓓ 12 for $39
    10 for $45

12. Read each sentence and select whether the rate is a rate or unit rate.

	Rate	Unit Rate
The earth rotates 1.25 degrees in 5 minutes.	○	○
Sarah reads 13 pages in 1/3 of an hour.	○	○
A man pays $45.24 for 16 gallons of gasoline.	○	○
The car drives 25 miles per hour.	○	○
The soup costs $1.23 per ounce.	○	○
40 millimeters of rain fell in 1 minute.	○	○

13. What is the unit rate for a pound of seed? Circle the correct answer choice.

Pounds of Seed	Total Cost
10	$17.50
20	$35.00
30	$52.50
40	$70.00

Ⓐ $3.50
Ⓑ $1.75
Ⓒ $17.50
Ⓓ $7.25

CHAPTER 2 → Lesson 7: Understanding and Representing Proportions

1. The following table shows two variables in a proportional relationship:

a	b
2	6
3	9
4	12

   Which of the following is an algebraic statement showing the relationship between a and b?

   Ⓐ a = 3b
   Ⓑ b = 3a
   Ⓒ b = 1/3 (a)
   Ⓓ a = 1/2 (b)

2. If the ratio of the length of a rectangle to its width is 3 to 2, what is the length of a rectangle whose width is 4 inches?

   Ⓐ 4 in.
   Ⓑ 5 in.
   Ⓒ 6 in.
   Ⓓ 7 in.

3. The following table shows two variables in a proportional relationship:

e	f
5	25
6	30
7	35

   Using the relationship between e and f as shown in this table, find the value of f when e = 11.

   Ⓐ 40
   Ⓑ 45
   Ⓒ 50
   Ⓓ 55

4. The following table shows two variables in a proportional relationship:

c	d
4	8
5	10
6	12

If c and d are proportional, then d = kc where k is the constant of proportionality.

Which of the following represents k in this case?

Ⓐ k = 1
Ⓑ k = 2
Ⓒ k = 3
Ⓓ k = 4

5. Ricky's family wants to invite his classroom to a "get acquainted" party. If 20 students attend the party then it will cost $100. Assuming the relationship between cost and guests is proportional, which of the following will be the cost if 29 students attend?

Ⓐ $129
Ⓑ $135
Ⓒ $139
Ⓓ $145

6. Which of the following pairs of ratios form a proportion?

Ⓐ 9 boys to 5 girls and 12 boys to 8 girls
Ⓑ 9 boys to 5 girls and 18 boys to 10 girls
Ⓒ 9 boys to 5 girls and 13 boys to 9 girls
Ⓓ 9 boys to 5 girls and 27 boys to 14 girls

7. If the local supermarket is selling oranges for *p* cents each and Mrs. Jones buys *n* oranges, write an equation for the total *(t)*, that Mrs. Jones pays for oranges.

Ⓐ t = p + n
Ⓑ t = p - n
Ⓒ t = pn
Ⓓ t = p/n

8. The ratio of Kathy's earnings to her hours worked is constant. This fact implies which of the following?

    Ⓐ Kathy's earnings are proportional to her hours of work.
    Ⓑ If Kathy works harder during her 8 hours of work today, her income for today will be greater than if she just takes it easy.
    Ⓒ If Kathy only works a half day today, her earnings will be the same as if she worked all day.
    Ⓓ If Kathy takes an extra hour for lunch, it will not affect her earnings for the day.

9. Write a mathematical statement (equation) for the relationship between feet and yards.

    Ⓐ number of feet / number of yards = 3
    Ⓑ number of yards / number of feet = 3
    Ⓒ number of feet - number of yards = 3
    Ⓓ number of feet + number of yards = 3

10. The ratio of the measurement of a length in yards to the measurement of the same length in feet is a constant. This implies that __?

    Ⓐ the measurement of a length in yards is directly proportional to the measurement of the same length in feet.
    Ⓑ the measurement in yards of a length is inversely proportional to the measurement of the same length in feet.
    Ⓒ the measurement in yards of a length is equivalent to the measurement of the same length in feet.
    Ⓓ There is no relationship between the two measurements.

11. Look at the table below. Decide whether the table shows a proportional relationship between x and y. Write Yes if the relationship is proportional or write No if the relationship is not proportional in the box given below.

x	2	4	7	10
y	4	16	49	100

12. Suppose you are buying pizzas for a party. An equation that represents the cost (y) in dollars for x number of pizzas is y=18x.

   Does the equation y=18x represent a proportional relationship? Instruction : Check all that are true

   Ⓐ No, the graph of the equation does not pass through the origin.
   Ⓑ Yes, the graph of the equation is a straight line
   Ⓒ Yes, the graph of the equation passes through the origin.
   Ⓓ No, the graph of the equation is not a straight line.

13. The table shows a proportional relationship between x and y. For each value of x and y, match it to the correct unit rate $\frac{y}{x}$ in it's simplest form.

	$\frac{6}{1}$	$\frac{3}{1}$	$\frac{9}{1}$
x = 3 and y = 27	☐	☐	☐
x = 9 and y = 81	☐	☐	☐
x = 21 and y = 126	☐	☐	☐
x = 14 and y = 84	☐	☐	☐
x = 12 and y = 36	☐	☐	☐
x = 15 and y = 45	☐	☐	☐

CHAPTER 2 → Lesson 8: Finding Constant of Proportionality

1. According to the graph, what is the constant of proportionality?

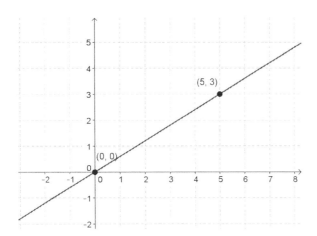

Ⓐ $\dfrac{3}{5}$

Ⓑ 5

Ⓒ 3

Ⓓ $\dfrac{1}{3}$

2. According to the table, how much does one ticket cost?

Number of Tickets	Total Cost
3	$ 21.00
4	$ 28.00
5	$ 35.00
6	$ 42.00

Ⓐ $21.00
Ⓑ $4.75
Ⓒ $7.00
Ⓓ $16.50

3. If y = 3x, what is the constant of proportionality between y and x?

   Ⓐ 1
   Ⓑ 0.30
   Ⓒ 1.50
   Ⓓ 3

4. When Frank buys three packs of pens, he knows he has 36 pens. When he buys five packs, he knows he has 60 pens. What is the constant of proportionality between the number of packs and the number of pens?

   Ⓐ 12
   Ⓑ 10
   Ⓒ 36
   Ⓓ 60

5. What is the unit rate for the number of hours of study each week per class?

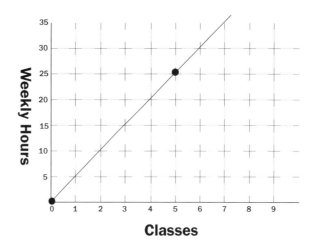

   Ⓐ 25 hours
   Ⓑ 5 hours
   Ⓒ 7 hours
   Ⓓ 10 hours

6. What is the constant of proportionality in the following equation?

   B = 1.25C

   Ⓐ 1.00
   Ⓑ 0.25
   Ⓒ 1.25
   Ⓓ 2.50

7. When Georgia buys 3 boxes of peaches, she has 40 pounds more than when she buys 1 box of peaches. How many pounds of peaches are in each box?

Ⓐ 40
Ⓑ 60
Ⓒ 20
Ⓓ 3

8. Look at the table below:

X	5	6	7	8
Y	90	108	126	144

What is the constant of proportionality of y to x? Enter your answer in the box given below.

9. Suppose the relationship between x and y is proportional. If the constant of proportionality of y to x is 16, select possible values for y and x.

Ⓐ x = 6 and y = 96
Ⓑ x = 96 and y = 6
Ⓒ x = 9 and y = 90
Ⓓ x = 144 and y = 9

10. In proportional relationships, there are dependent and independent variables. Match each situation to whether it is an independent variable or not.

	Independent Variable	Dependent Variable
The number of concert tickets sold is based on how many hours the ticket booth is open. What kind of variable is the number of hours the ticket booth is open?	☐	☐
The number of cans that is collected for a charity drive is based on how many students bring in cans. What kind of variable is the number of students?	☐	☐
The number of buses needed for a field trip depends on how many students are going on the field trip. What kind of variable is the number of buses?	☐	☐
The number of cell phone towers built is determined by how many customers are in the area. What kind of variable is the number of cell phone towers?	☐	☐

CHAPTER 2 → Lesson 9: Significance of Points on Graphs of Proportions

1. **Which point on the graph of the straight line demonstrates that the line represents a proportion?**

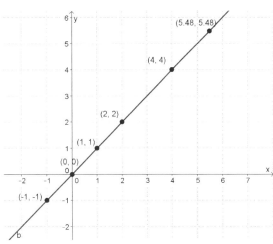

Ⓐ (2, 2)
Ⓑ (0, 0)
Ⓒ (5.48, 5.48)
Ⓓ (-1, -1)

2. **Which point on the graph of the straight line names the unit rate of the proportional relationship?**

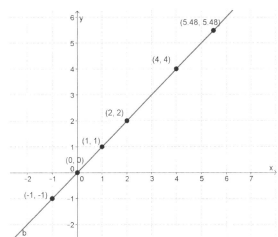

Ⓐ (1, 1)
Ⓑ (0, 0)
Ⓒ (2, 2)
Ⓓ (4, 4)

3. The graph shows the relationship between the number of classes in the school and the total number of students. How many students are there per class?

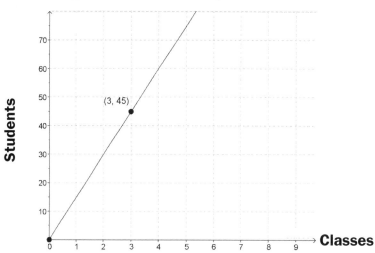

Ⓐ 45 students
Ⓑ 3 students
Ⓒ 135 students
Ⓓ 15 students

4. Use the information given on the graph to find the value of y.

Ⓐ 30
Ⓑ 5
Ⓒ 10
Ⓓ 11

5. In order for the relationship to be proportional, what other point must be a part of the graph?

  Ⓐ (5, 10)
  Ⓑ (5, 25)
  Ⓒ (5, 15)
  Ⓓ (5, 20)

6. What is the unit rate of Birthday presents per child?

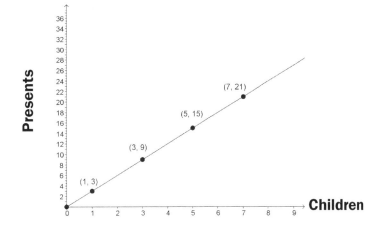

  Ⓐ 21 presents
  Ⓑ 9 presents
  Ⓒ 3 presents
  Ⓓ 15 presents

7. **What is the unit rate of bushels of apples per tree?**

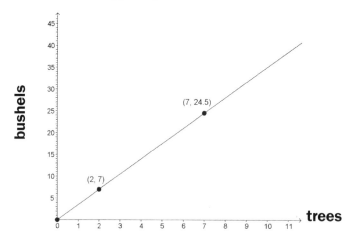

Ⓐ 3.5
Ⓑ 7
Ⓒ 24.5
Ⓓ 14

8. **Which point represents the profit if no boxes of popcorn are sold for the fundraiser?**

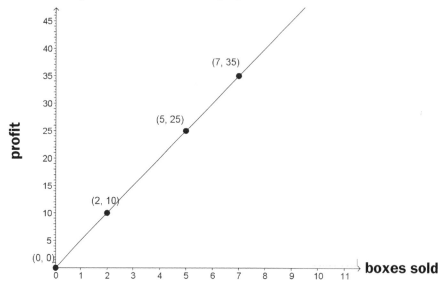

Ⓐ (5, 25)
Ⓑ (7, 35)
Ⓒ (0, 0)
Ⓓ (2, 10)

9. If the relationship between x and y is proportional, what point on the line will indicate the unit rate of that relationship?

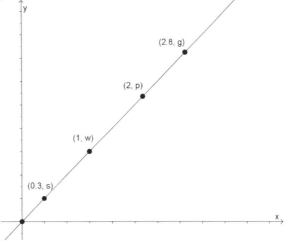

Ⓐ (2, p)
Ⓑ (0.3, s)
Ⓒ (2.8, g)
Ⓓ (1, w)

10. According to the information given on the graph, how much would 20 boards cost?

Ⓐ $200
Ⓑ $400
Ⓒ $80
Ⓓ $120

11. Does this graph represent a proportional relationship? Enter your answer as "Yes" or "No" in the box given below.

12. What do the points on the graph mean? Select all the correct answers.

Ⓐ After 2 weeks, you have saved $94
Ⓑ After 94 weeks, you have saved $2
Ⓒ After 10 weeks, you have saved $94
Ⓓ After 4 weeks, you have saved $188
Ⓔ After 0 weeks, you have saved $10

13. Match the situations to the corresponding graphs.

	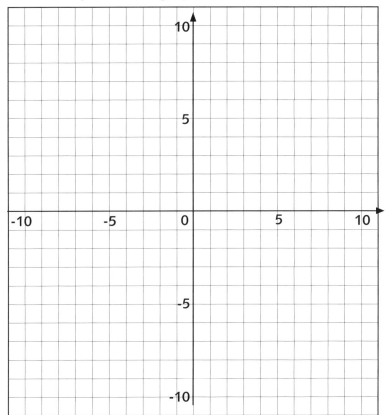	
Jake ran 3 km in 9 minutes.	○	○
Sara walked 3 feet in 30 seconds.	○	○
After 1 minute, the turtle had traveled 6 feet.	○	○
It took Roger 15 minutes to walk 5 km.	○	○

14. Plot the points (0,0) and (1,4) on the graph. In order for the relationship to be proportional, what other point must be a part of the graph.

CHAPTER 2 → Lesson 10: Represent Proportions by Equations

1. **3 hats cost a total of $18. Which equation describes the total cost, C, in terms of the number of hats, n?**

   Ⓐ $C = 3n$
   Ⓑ $C = 6n$
   Ⓒ $C = 0.5n$
   Ⓓ $3C = n$

2. **Use the data in the table to give an equation to represent the proportional relationship.**

x	y
0.5	7
1	14
1.5	21
2	28

   Ⓐ $y = 14x$
   Ⓑ $y = 7x$
   Ⓒ $7y = x$
   Ⓓ $21y = x$

3. **Kelli has purchased a membership at the gym for the last four months. She has paid the same amount each month, and her total cost so far has been $100. What equation expresses the proportional relationship of the cost and month?**

   Ⓐ $C = 100m$
   Ⓑ $C = 50m$
   Ⓒ $C = 4m$
   Ⓓ $C = 25m$

4. **When buying bananas at the market, Marco pays $4.50 for 5 pounds. What is the relationship between pounds, p, and cost, C?**

   Ⓐ $C = 4.5p$
   Ⓑ $C = 5p$
   Ⓒ $C = 0.9p$
   Ⓓ $C = 22.5p$

5. The cost to rent an apartment is proportional to the number of square feet in the apartment. An 800 square foot apartment costs $600 per month. What equation represents the relationship between area, a, and cost, C?

    (A) C = 0.75a
    (B) C = 1.33a
    (C) C = 8a
    (D) C = 6a

6. A school has to purchase new desks for their classrooms. They have to purchase 350 new desks, and they pay $7000. What equation demonstrates the relationship between the number of desks, d, and the total cost, C?

    (A) C = 10d
    (B) C = 20d
    (C) C = 70d
    (D) C = 35d

7. A soccer club is hosting a tournament with 12 teams involved. Each team has a set number of players, and there are a total of 180 players involved in the tournament. Which equation represents the proportional relationship between teams, t, and players, p?

    (A) p = 15t
    (B) p = 12t
    (C) p = 18t
    (D) p = 11t

8. A package of three rolls of tape costs $5 per pack. What is the proportional relationship between cost, C, and package of tape, p?

    (A) C = 1.67p
    (B) C = 15p
    (C) C = 3p
    (D) C = 5p

9. Freddy is building a house and has 5 loads of gravel delivered for the work. His total cost for the gravel is $1750. Which equation correctly shows the relationship between cost, C, and loads of gravel, g?

    (A) C = 5g
    (B) C = 350g
    (C) C = 75g
    (D) C = 225g

10. Use the graph to write an equation for the proportional relationship between the number of hours Corrie works, h, and her total pay, P.

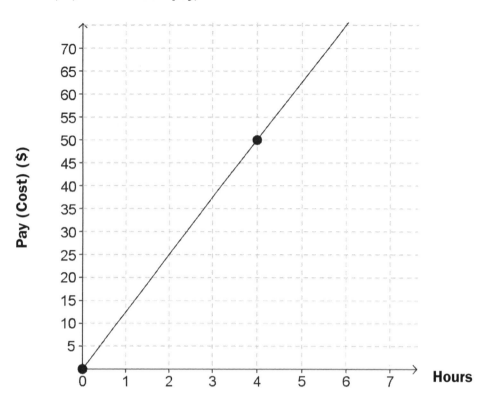

Ⓐ P = 12.50h
Ⓑ P = 50h
Ⓒ P = 4h
Ⓓ P = 22.50h

11. You run 9.1 miles in 1.3 hours at a steady rate. Write an equation that represents the proportional relationship between the x hours you run and the distance y in miles that you travel? Write the equation in the box given below

12. Sally paid $3.50 for 7 apples. Write an equation to represent the total cost y of buying x apples.

   Instruction: Select the correct equation to describe the situation. There may be more than one correct answer.

   Ⓐ y = 7x
   Ⓑ 3.50y = x
   Ⓒ y = 0.50x
   Ⓓ x = 7
   Ⓔ y = 3.50x
   Ⓕ $y = \dfrac{3.50}{7}x$

13. Solve each proportion for x and match it with the correct solution for x.

	x = 9	x = 10	x = 7
$\dfrac{x}{15} = \dfrac{3}{5}$	☐	☐	☐
$\dfrac{16}{14} = \dfrac{8}{x}$	☐	☐	☐
$\dfrac{4}{20} = \dfrac{2}{x}$	☐	☐	☐
$\dfrac{75}{x} = \dfrac{50}{6}$	☐	☐	☐

End of Algebraic Reasoning

Chapter 2
Algebraic Reasoning

Lesson 1: Applying Properties to Rational Expressions

Question No.	Answer	Detailed Explanations
1	A	Remember: "Younger than" is a key phrase that will indicate subtraction. If A is the age of Ruby's brother, and she is 2 years younger than her brother. The correct expression is A - 2.
2	C	8n - (3n-6) = 8n - 3n + 6 = 5n + 6. 5n + 6 is the correct answer.
3	A	6t + (3t - 5) = Remove parentheses: 6t + (3t − 5) = 6t + 3t - 5. Now combine like terms: 6t + 3t − 5 = 9t − 5. 9t - 5 is the correct answer.
4	B	7x - 14x + 21x - 2. Here, I will combine like terms first. 7x - 14x + 21x = 14x. Now we have 14x − 2, which factors into 2(7x - 1). 2(7x - 1) is the correct answer.

5	A	Simplify the expression 3(x + 4) - 2
		Step 1: Multiply terms in parentheses by 3
		  3x+12-2
		Step 2: Combine like terms
		  3x+10

6	A	Simplify the expression $(\frac{1}{2})x + (\frac{3}{2})x$ Add the numerators of the fractions and keep the same denominators $(\frac{4}{2})x$ Simplify this fraction we get 2x.
7	A	Simplify the expression 0.25x + 3 - 0.5x + 2 by combining like terms Step 1: 0.25x - 0.5x + 3 + 2 Step 2: -0.25x + 5
8	C	Remember: Addition means more than and 2x represents multiplication, or times. The statement that represents the expression 2x + 4 is four more than two times a number.

Question No.	Answer	Detailed Explanations
9	A	Remember: A half can be represented by the fraction $\frac{1}{2}$, twice indicates multiplication, and less represents subtraction. Considering the numerator (2x-3), means 3 less than twice a number 'x'. Dividing this by half, we get half of three less than twice a number.
10	D	Simplify the expression $\frac{1}{2}$ (2x + 4) - 3 Step 1: Multiply terms in parentheses by $\frac{1}{2}$ (x+2) - 3 Step 2: Combine like terms (x - 1)
11	B	Distributive property is the correct answer. To remove parentheses, we must multiply the quantity outside parentheses to each term inside parentheses.
12	D	Perimeter = 2 • length + 2 • width 2(4x + 9) + 2(3x - 5) = 8x + 18 + 6x - 10 = 14x +8 ft. 14x + 8 is the correct answer.
13	C	5280 ft ÷ (5x + 3) ft represents the number of laps in 1 mile. 5280 / (5x + 3) is the correct answer.
14	B	5x + 10y + 0(z) = 5x + 10y When 0 is multiplied by any quantity, it produces 0; so 0(z) = 0. Then 5x + 10y + 0 = 5x + 10y 5x + 10y is the correct answer.
15	D	The associative property of addition states that the sum of 3 or more numbers is the same regardless how the numbers are grouped.
16	30x - 18	Distribute the six by multiplying 6 and 5x. Then multiply 6 by 3. Subtract the two products.
17	D, E, and F	D, E, and F are the correct options. Find a common factor between 60 and 24. Some common factors are 6 and 4. Divide the two numbers in the expression by the common factor. 60 divided by 6 is 10 and 24 divided by 6 is 4. Also 60 divided by 4 is 15 and 24 divided by 4 is 6. -6 can be a factor if you make sure to change the 10 to negative and the subtraction sign to a +.
18	$88	p=13 so 8(13-2) = 88.

Lesson 2: Interpreting the Meanings of Expressions

Question No.	Answer	Detailed Explanations
1	C	A percent is a ratio that compares a number to 100. Therefore, 5% is 5 out of 100. To convert a percent to a decimal, divide by 100: 5 ÷ 100 = 0.05. To find 5% of a number, multiply the number times the decimal form of 5%: 0.05n. 0.05n is the correct answer.
2	C	SP = RP - 0.15(RP), SP = RP(1 - 0.15), SP = RP(0.85), SP = 0.85 RP is the correct answer.
3	D	P = l + w + l + w Combine like terms. P = 2(l) + 2(w) Factor out 2. P = 2(l + w) is the correct answer.
4	B	Percentage of the sale price = [profit ÷ sale price],100 = [(y - x) ÷ y], 100 = 100(y - x)/y is the correct answer.
5	C	(x + x + 1+ x + 2 + x + 3 + x + 4) / 5 = Average (a) (5x + 10) / 5 = x + 2. x + 2 is the correct answer.
6	B	0.10 ($ (d + 5) - $ d) = 0.10 (d + 5 - d)= 0.10(5) $0.50 is the correct answer.
7	A	$(\frac{30-18}{30})$ n = $(\frac{12}{30})$ n = $(\frac{2}{5})$ n days is the correct answer.
8	D	r = m /[(20 + 10 +15) / 60] r = m / $(\frac{45}{60})$ = m / $(\frac{3}{4})$ = $\frac{4m}{3}$ mph
9	A	During week 5n, Hannah must practice $1+\frac{1}{2}$(5n -1). $1 +\frac{5n - 1}{2}$ = $\frac{2}{2}$ + $\frac{5n - 1}{2}$ = $\frac{2+5n-1}{2}$ = $\frac{1 + 5n}{2}$ is the correct answer.
10	A	Scientific notation is a simpler way to compute with very large or very small numbers. Using scientific notation, 1,400,000 km = 1.4×10^6 km 1.4×10^6 km is the correct answer.
11	D	(6x - 15y - 2x + y) / -4(x - y) = (4x - 14y) / -4(x - y) = 2(2x - 7y) / -4(x - y) = (2x - 7y) / - 2(x - y) is the correct answer.
12	B	If n is any number, and that number is increased by 24%, finding that increase means multiplying that number by 24% and then adding the product to the original number. Therefore, the expression n + 0.24n represents a 24% increase.

Question No.	Answer	Detailed Explanations
13	D	Team A score -19 = Team B score Add 19 to both sides of the equation. Team A Score -19 + 19 = Team B Score + 19 Team A Score = Team B Score + 19 is the correct answer.
14	A	Cost / yd = [3($6.99)] / 3[3(50) + 3(25)] = $20.97/675 yd = $0.031/yd is the correct answer.
15	D	Cost/lb=$40(50)/[50(50) + 5(50)] Cost/lb =[$40(50)]/[55(50)] lb Cost/lb = $\dfrac{\$40(50)}{55(50)}$ lb is the correct answer.
16	0.85p	p is the same as 1p. Therefore 1p - 0.15p = 0.85p.
17	B, C and E	B, C and E are correct options. The following are not like terms: 4xy - 8y (are not like because xy is not the same variable as y) 5t + 5 (5 is a constant and not a variable) 8x - 2y (x and y are different variables)

Lesson 3: Linear Inequality Word Problems

Question No.	Answer	Detailed Explanations
1	C	3000 must be multiplied by y, the years of experience. This amount must then be added to the base salary of $50,000. This sum must be less than or equal to $70,000.
2	B	The weekly increase of 45 is multiplied by the number of weeks. This amount is added to the initial savings of 225. This sum must be greater than or equal to 500.
3	D	The number of minutes of charging time must be multiplied by 2 and divided by 3 to find the percentage of the battery that is charged over that time. This is then added to the initial charge of 20 percent, and the sum must be at least 75.
4	A	Set up an inequality that $74 + 0.20t \geq 90$. Solving for t, we find that $t \geq 80$.
5	C	Set up an inequality that $100 - 4n \geq 83$. Solving for n, we find that $n \leq 4.25$. Because you can only miss whole numbers of problems, the most he can miss is 4.
6	B	In the inequality, let T be 12, and solve for L. $12 \geq 3 + 0.2L$ ($\geq$ is to be read as greater than or equal to and $\leq$ as less than or equal to). $9 \geq 0.2L$ or $L \leq 9/0.2$ or $L \leq 45$. Therefore Maximum unsupported length for a panel of thickness 12 mm is 45 ft.
7	C	If the number of units sold is 0, the 300 is still present as the minimum amount of the pay. The 25 is multiplied by 0 in the equation and thus negated, but the 300 remains.
8	B	$C = 750 - 200h$. If $h = 3.75$, $C = 750 - (200 \times 3.75) = 750 - 750 = 0$ So, if Neil does 3.75 hours of exercise in a week, he will not gain weight. If he does exercise for more than 3.75 hours, he will lose weight.
9	B	Because there are twice as many girls as boys to be admitted, girls must make up $\frac{2}{3}$ of the admitted group. This leaves one third to be boys. One third of 300 is 100.
10	A	His minimum hours of chores increased by 1.5 hours. This must represent 6 hours of TV watching that week .

Question No.	Answer	Detailed Explanations
11	6 hrs	Write the inequality to be: 5 + 2x is less than or equal to 17. Subtract 5 from each side and divide by 2 to get 6. x≤6 . So, Liz can rent a bike almost for 6 hours.
12	D and E	D and E are correct options. Let p be the cost of a popsicle. The cost of an ice cream cone is 2p and the cost of a double scoop is 3p. So, 2p + 2(2p) + 2(3p) = 12p. 12p is less than 24.12. Divide each side by 12 and p has to be less than $2.01.
13	B	The flower trays added up have to be more than 200. So, Option (B) is correct.

Lesson 4: Modeling Using Equations or Inequalities

Question No.	Answer	Detailed Explanations
1	D	The first step to solving this problem is to figure out the value of t, the number of hours. As you know, 7 am to 3 pm represents 5 hours to 12 pm, then another 3 hours to 3pm, for a total of 8 hours. This gives us W = 3.75(8) = 30, a full tank.
2	D	Let the volume of water = w and volume of milk = m. $m/w = 3/8$. Rearranging the above equation, $m = \frac{3w}{8}$, $m + w = 187$ cubic ft. Replacing the value of m by $\frac{3w}{8}$ in the above equation, $\frac{3w}{8} + w = 187$, $\frac{11w}{8} = 187$, $w = \frac{187*8}{11} = 136$ cubic ft.
3	D	Remember: The volume of a rectangular box is V = lwh. This lets us set up the following equation: 960 = 12(10)h, 960 = 120h, 8 = h This gives us a height of 8 inches, as indicated.
4	D	Let b = the number of bushels harvested $\frac{24}{12} = \frac{18}{b}$, 24b = 12(18), 24b = 216, b = 9 bushels is the correct answer.
5	C	Let m = Melanie's age; Then 27-m = Roni's Age; m - (27-m) = 3; m - 27 + m = 3; 2m - 27 = 3; 2m = 3 + 27; 2m = 30; m = $\frac{30}{2}$ = 15 years = Melanie's Age; Roni's Age = 27-m = 27-15 = 12 yrs. Alternative Explanation: Among the options, guess in which case the difference in age is 3 years. It is clear that option (C) is the correct answer.
6	B	Solving this problem requires the creation of a simple equation: 2.5(x) = 50 Dividing 50 by 2.5, the answer is 20.
7	B	11 + (8 + 6) = (y + 8) + 6 This equation demonstrates the associative property for addition, which states that when adding three or more quantities, the way that they are grouped does not affect the sum. Therefore, y = 11 because of the associative property of addition.
8	C	p = 2c + 1, p = 2(7) + 1, p = 14 + 1, p = 15 people present 15 is the correct answer.

Question No.	Answer	Detailed Explanations
9	A	Let the volume of salt = x and volume of sugar = y. $\frac{x}{y} = \frac{4}{8}$. Rearranging the above equation, $x = \frac{4y}{8} = \frac{y}{2}$. $x + y = 300$ cubic ft. Replacing the value of x by $\frac{y}{2}$ in the above equation, $\frac{y}{2} + y = 300$. $\frac{3y}{2} = 300$. $y = \frac{(300*2)}{3}$. $y = 200$ cubic ft.
10	A	Apply the rule to each number's position in the sequence: (1) $(8 + 1^2) - 2 \times 1 = 7$, (2) $(8 + 2^2) - 2 \times 2 = 8$, (3) $(8 + 3^2) - 2 \times 3 = 11$, (4) $(8 + 4^2) - 2 \times 4 = 16$, (5) $(8 + 5^2) - 2 \times 5 = 23$. Therefore, sequence 7, 8, 11, 16, 23, ... follows the rule $(8 + t^2) - 2t$.
11	x = 6	The equation is $x + 4 = 10$. Subtract 4 from both sides and get $x = 6$.
12	A and D	A and D are correct options. The model shows that 2 x's equals 14 ones. So $2x = 14$ or $x + x = 14$. To solve, divide both sides by 2 and get $x = 7$.

Lesson 5: Applying Ratios and Percents

Question No.	Answer	Detailed Explanations
1	D	In a set of equivalent ratios, or a proportion, the numerator and denominator of one ratio will be multiplied by the same number to get the values of the other ratio. In this case, the denominator of the first ratio, 7, is multiplied by 3 to get to 21. This means (-3) must also be multiplied by 3 to get to (-9).
2	A	To find the constant of proportionality, find the relationship between p and s. When p = 10 and s = 2, dividing p by s shows that p is 5 times s. Therefore, the equation that shows the constant of proportionality is p = 5s.
3	B	To solve this proportion for x, multiply both sides of the equation by 54, and simplify the result, We get, x = 36.
4	B	To find the constant of proportionality, find the relationship between s and d. s is 75% of d, which is the same as 0.75 times d. Therefore, the equation that shows the constant of proportionality is s = 0.75d.
5	D	Set up a proportion between the known ratio and the unknown ratio, and solve for y. $$\frac{6}{4} = \frac{9}{y}$$ $6y = 9\,(4)$ Cross Multiply $6y = 36$ Simplify $\dfrac{6y}{6} = \dfrac{36}{6}$ Divide each side by 6 $y = 6$ Simplify
6	B	Selling price (sp) = Original price (op) - 0.30(op) sp = 250 - 0.30(250) sp = 250 - 75 sp = 175. $175 is the correct answer.
7	B	Original price (op) - 0.15(op) = Selling price (sp) op - 0.15(op) = 110.49 0.85(op) = 110.49 $$op = \frac{110.49}{0.85}$$ op = $129.99. $129.99 is the correct answer.

Question No.	Answer	Detailed Explanations
8	C	Using original measurements, Area=1300 x 982=1,276,600 sq ft. Using actual measurements, Area=1285 x 982=1,261,870 sq ft. Error = 14,730 sq ft. $\dfrac{14,730}{1,276,600} \times 100 = 1.15\%$ error. The correct answer is 1.15%. Alternate Explanation : Since width is same in both the cases, we can write error $=\dfrac{(\text{original length x width}) - (\text{measured length x width})}{(\text{original length x width})}$ $=\dfrac{(1300 \times 982) - (1285 \times 982)}{(1300 \times 982)} = 982$ $\dfrac{1300 - 1285}{1300 \times 982}$. Since 982 is common factor in both numerator and denominator, error $=\dfrac{1300 - 1285}{1300} = \dfrac{15}{1300} = 0.0115 = 1.15\%$
9	D	\$36.00 - \$22.00 = \$14.00 in fees. $\dfrac{\$14.00}{\$22.00} = \dfrac{14}{22} = \dfrac{7}{11}$ is the ratio of fees to the cost of the ticket. $\dfrac{7}{11}$ is the correct answer.
10	B	Selling price - cost = markup \$73.50 - \$42.00 = \$31.50 markup markup / (cost - percent of markup) $\dfrac{\$31.50}{\$42} = 0.75 = 75\%$ markup. The correct answer is 75%.
11	19.2	64 times 0.30=19.2. Use the percent equation: part=percent times whole.
12	B and C	B and C are correct options. 60% of 54 is 32.4 (0.60*54=32.4) 60% of 5 is 3 (0.60*5=3)

13

	Part	Percent	Whole
What is 35% of 15?	☐		
4% of what number is 46?			☐
y = .76 × 43	☐		
14 = m × 56	☐		

Use the percent equation to solve. Part = percent times whole. The word "what" tells you what the question is looking for.

Lesson 6: Unit Rates

Question No.	Answer	Detailed Explanations
1	B	First, find out the area of the tennis court. (1) $25 \times 20 = 500$ square feet Next, find out the area of one plastic cover (2) $13 \times 10 = 130$ square feet Divide 500 by 130 (3) $500 \div 130 = 3.84$ Therefore, 4 plastic covers are needed for the tennis court.
2	A	First, find out how much cereal John eats in 8 days: (1) 3 bowls per day x 8 days = 24 bowls. Since it takes 2 gallons of milk to eat 24 bowls of cereal, set up the ratio and simplify: (2) $\frac{2}{24}$ (GCF is 2, so divide numerator and denominator to find simplest form) (3) $\frac{1}{12}$ Therefore, John uses $\frac{1}{12}$ of a gallon of milk in each bowl of cereal.
3	C	To solve this problem, first, find the amount of milk required for each layer. For the first layer, $\frac{3}{4}$ cup of milk is required. Since the second layer is half the size, the amount of milk required will be $\frac{3}{4} \times \frac{1}{2} = \frac{3}{8}$ cups are required. For the third layer, which is half of layer two, the milk required will be $\frac{3}{8} \times \frac{1}{2} = \frac{3}{16}$ of a cup. The total milk required will be $\frac{3}{4} + \frac{3}{8} + \frac{3}{16}$ To add, find the LCD, which is 16 in this case. Hence, $\frac{3}{4} + \frac{3}{8} + \frac{3}{16}$ represented by LCD will become $(\frac{3}{4} \times \frac{4}{4}) + (\frac{3}{8} \times \frac{2}{2}) + \frac{3}{16}$ $= \frac{12}{16} + \frac{6}{16} + \frac{3}{16} = \frac{21}{16}$ Converting this to mixed fraction we get, $1\frac{5}{16}$. Hence, the correct answer choice is Option C.

Question No.	Answer	Detailed Explanations
4	A	If $\frac{1}{4}$ th of a basketball court can be covered by $\frac{1}{3}$ rd of a quart of paint then to cover the entire court 4 times the amount required for covering $\frac{1}{4}$ th of a court would be required. Therefore, Paint required to cover the entire court $= \frac{1}{3} \times 4 = \frac{4}{3} = 1\frac{1}{3}$
5	C	Unit price means price per one unit. Therefore, we need to know the price per pencil. Since the price of the pencils is defined to be a constant rate, then the total cost ($39.00) divided by the total number of pencils (100) will give us the cost per pencil (or per unit). $39.00 / 100 = $0.39 per pencil The unit price is $0.39. The correct answer is $0.39.
6	B	To solve this problem, find out how much it takes to cover 1/5 of the wall, and then multiply by 5. (1) $50 \div 3 =$ (how much it takes to cover 1/5 of the bathroom wall) (2) multiply $16.66 \times 5 = 83.33$ (3) $83.33 = 83\frac{1}{3}$ Therefore, it will take 83 and one-third tiles to cover the entire wall.
7	B	To solve this problem, set up a proportion: (distance)/(time) = (distance)/(time) Plug in the numbers (you can convert to decimals to simplify the process): $\frac{0.8 \text{ mile}}{x \text{ min}} = \frac{12 \text{ miles}}{60 \text{ min}}$. Using cross products $a/b = c/d$ is $ad = bc$ $(0.8)(60) = (x)(12)$ $48 = 12x$ (solve for x by dividing each side by 12) $4 = x$. Therefore, Jim ran 4 minutes.
8	B	To solve this problem, multiply $\frac{3}{4} \times 3\frac{1}{2}$ (1). Convert $3\frac{1}{2}$ to an improper fraction $= \frac{7}{2}$ (2) $\frac{3}{4} \times \frac{7}{2} =$ (3) $\frac{3 \times 7}{4 \times 2} =$ (4) $\frac{21}{8}$ (convert back to a mixed number)(5) $2\frac{5}{8}$ (6) $\frac{5}{8} = 37.5$ minutes. Therefore, Ping played 2 hours 37 minutes and 30 seconds.

Question No.	Answer	Detailed Explanations
9	B	To answer the question we must find in which case he ran the most steps per minute.
		Since he is running up and down, we double the number of steps; so
		$\dfrac{50}{5} = 10$ steps per minute
		$\dfrac{60}{5.5} = 10.9$ steps per minute * (when rounded to the nearest tenth)
		$\dfrac{40}{4.5} = 8.9$ steps per minute (when rounded to the nearest tenth)
		$\dfrac{30}{4} = 7.5$ steps per minute
		30 steps in 5.5 minutes gives an average of 10.9 steps per minute which is his best time.
		30 steps in 5.5 minutes is the correct answer.
		(Note : If we don't double the steps, then also answer does not change. Only the number of steps per minute will differ)
10	B	To solve this problem, set up a proportion: (distance)/(time) = (distance)/(time) $\dfrac{1}{3}$ of an hour is equivalent to 20 minutes. Plug in the numbers (you can convert to decimals to simplify the process): $\dfrac{30.33 \text{ miles}}{20 \text{ minutes}} = \dfrac{100 \text{ miles}}{x \text{ minutes}}$. Using cross products a/b = c/d is ad = bc
		$(30.33)(x) = (20)(100)$
		$30.33x = 2000$ (solve for x by dividing each side by 30.33) x = 65.94 (round up to the nearest whole number). Since 65.94 is almost 66 minutes, that is the same as one hour and 6 minutes.
11	A and D	A and D are correct options. $26 divided by 8 = $3.25 $39 divided by 12 = $3.25 $30 divided by 5 = $6 $15 divided by 4 = $3.75 $45 divided by 10 = $4.50 So the best deal is the deal where the unit cost is the lowest. Therefore the two deals where the unit rates are $3.25 is the correct answer.

Question No.	Answer	Detailed Explanations
12		

	Rate	Unit Rate
The earth rotates 1.25 degrees in 5 minutes.	●	○
Sarah reads 13 pages in 1/3 of an hour.	●	○
A man pays $45.24 for 16 gallons of gasoline.	●	○
The car drives 25 miles per hour.	○	●
The soup costs $1.23 per ounce.	○	●
40 millimeters of rain fell in 1 minute.	○	●

The unit rates are rates that reflect amounts per 1 unit. Rates are comparisons of two amounts that are not zero.

Question No.	Answer	Detailed Explanations
13	B	For any of the pairs of data, divide the total cost by the number of pounds of seed to find how much one pound costs. For example, $17.50/10 = $1.75 per pound.

Lesson 7: Understanding and Representing Proportions

Question No.	Answer	Detailed Explanations
1	B	In each case, if we multiply a by 3, we get b. b = 3a is the correct answer.
2	C	We know that, length/width $= \dfrac{3}{2}$ The width is given as 4 inches, Hence, we get, $\dfrac{3}{2} = \dfrac{x}{4}$ where x is the length. Cross multiplying we get, $x = \dfrac{3 \times 4}{2}$ $x = \dfrac{12}{2} = 6$ in Hence, Option C is the correct answer choice.
3	D	The table shows that f = 5e, then 5 is the constant of proportionality. Therefore, f = 5e; so if e = 11, f = 5 x 11 = 55. Hence, 55 is the correct answer.
4	B	In each case, d = 2c. Therefore, k = 2. 2 is the constant of proportionality. k = 2 is the correct answer.
5	D	Since the relationship is proportional we can write the mathematical statement, $\dfrac{20}{100}$ = 29/c. So 20c = 2900. c = $145. $145 is the correct answer.
6	B	A proportion consists of two equivalent ratios. $\dfrac{9}{5} = \dfrac{18}{10}$ because 9 x 10 = 5 x 18. 9 boys to 5 girls and 18 boys to 10 girls is the correct answer.
7	C	In this case, p is constant regardless of the number, n, of oranges that she buys. To find the total cost, t, we multiply the number of oranges purchased, n, by the cost per orange, p. t = pn is the correct answer.
8	A	If Kathy's earnings are proportional to her hours of work, then the ratio of her earnings to hours worked is a constant. "Kathy's earnings are proportional to her hours of work" is the correct answer.
9	A	Since 3 ft = 1 yd, if we divide feet by yards, the quotient will always be 3. "number of feet / number of yards = 3" is the correct answer.
10	A	Since these ratios are always equivalent to a constant, the variables are directly proportional by definition. "The measurement in yards of a length is directly proportional to the measurement of the same length in feet" is the correct answer.

Question No.	Answer	Detailed Explanations
11	No	The table shows a relationship that is not proportional because the relationship between x and y is not constant. For example, when x=2 and y=4, the constant of proportionality is 2. However, when x=4 and y=16, the constant of proportionality is 4. There is a relationship between x and y but it is not proportional.
12	B and C	B and C are correct options. One can check whether or not an equation of a line represents a proportional relationship by observing whether the equation represents a straight line and whether the line passes through the origin. The correct answer is that yes, the equation represents a proportional relationship because the graph is a straight line and also because it passes through the origin.
13		

	$\dfrac{6}{1}$	$\dfrac{3}{1}$	$\dfrac{9}{1}$
x = 3 and y = 27	☐	☐	■
x = 9 and y = 81	☐	☐	■
x = 21 and y = 126	■	☐	☐
x = 14 and y = 84	■	☐	☐
x = 12 and y = 36	☐	■	☐
x = 15 and y = 45	☐	■	☐

To determine the ratio $\dfrac{Y}{X}$ you should divide y by x or simplify the fraction to simplest form. Each of the items match only one of the three ratios at the top of the table.

Lesson 8: Finding Constant of Proportionality

Question No.	Answer	Detailed Explanations
1	A	The line passes through the origin, so it is a proportional relationship. The second point gives the constant of proportionality, which is the y value divided by the x value: $\frac{3}{5}$.
2	C	For any of the pairs of data, divide the total cost by the number of tickets to find how much one ticket costs. For example, $\frac{\$21}{3} = \$7$ per ticket.
3	D	Because the equation is solved for y and is equal to a multiple of x, the coefficient of the x term gives the constant of proportionality: 3.
4	A	Divide the number of pens by the number of packs for either pair of data. For example, $\frac{36}{3} = 12$ pens per pack.
5	B	The line passes through the origin, so it is a proportional relationship. The second point gives the constant of proportionality, which is the y value divided by the x value: $\frac{25}{5}$, which simplifies to 5.
6	C	Because the equation is solved for y and is equal to a multiple of x, the coefficient of the x term gives the constant of proportionality: 1.25.
7	C	The difference between our two pairs of data is 2 boxes and 40 pounds of peaches. Divide the difference in pounds by the difference in boxes: $\frac{40}{2} = 20$ pounds per box.
8	18	The constant of proportionality is 18 because the relationship between x and y is to multiply by 18. For example, 5x18=90, 6x18=108, 7x18=126, 8x18=144. You can find this by dividing y by x.
9	A	The constant of proportionality of y to x is determined by dividing y by x. Because $\frac{96}{6} = 16$.

Question No.	Answer	Detailed Explanations
10		The number of hours the ticket booth is open is an independent variable because the number of tickets sold is dependent on the number of hours the ticket booth is open. The number of cell phone towers built is the dependent variable because the number of cell phone towers built is determined by how many customers are in the area. The number of buses is the dependent Variable because the number of buses depends on how many students are going on the field trip. The number of students who bring in cans is the independent variable because the number of cans collected is based on how many students bring in cans.

Lesson 9: Significance of Points on Graphs of Proportions

Question No.	Answer	Detailed Explanations
1	B	A straight line graph is a proportion if and only if it passes through the origin, (0, 0).
2	A	The unit rate is the amount per single unit of something. This means that the point located at 1 on the x-axis will indicate the unit rate: (1, 1).
3	D	Find the unit rate, which is the number of students per one class, by dividing the y value by the x value for the given point: $\frac{45}{3} = 15$ students per class.
4	A	The unit rate shows that y is 6 times the value of x. Multiply the x value of 5 by 6, and 30 is the value of y.
5	D	The unit rate is given by the point (1, 4). y must be 4 times x. That relationship is found only in the point (5, 20).
6	C	The unit rate is found at the point where x has a value of 1. That point is (1, 3), so the unit rate is 3 presents per child.
7	A	The unit rate can be found by dividing the y value by the x value for any given point: $\frac{7}{2} = 3.5$ bushels per tree.
8	C	The point (0, 0) always represents the origin of the proportion. In this case, that means that no boxes are sold, and the profit will be $0.
9	D	The unit rate is always located at the point where the x value is 1. In this case, that is (1, w).
10	A	The unit rate is found at (1, 10), which indicates that 1 board has a cost of $10. Multiply by 20 boards to find the total cost: (10)(20) = $200.
11	Yes	Yes it does because it is a straight line that passes through the origin.
12	A and D	A and D are the correct options. You use the x and y coordinates to determine the meaning of the points. The point (2,94) means that after two weeks you have saved $94. The point (4,188) means that after 4 weeks you have saved $188.

13		
	Jake ran 3 km in 9 minutes.	● ○
	Sara walked 3 feet in 30 seconds.	○ ●
	After 1 minute, the turtle had traveled 6 feet.	○ ●
	It took Roger 15 minutes to walk 5 km.	● ○

Jake ran 3 km in 9 minutes describes the point (9,3). Sara walked 3 feet in 30 seconds describes the point (0.5,3). After 1 minute, the turtle had traveled 6 feet describes the point (1,6). It took Roger 15 minutes to walk 5 km describes (15,5).

| 14 | Coordinates are represented as (x,y)
(0,0) means 0 on x axis and 0 on y axis
(1,4) means 1 on x axis and 4 on y axis.

Plot the points.
The unit rate is given by the point (1, 4). y must be 4 times x, y = 4x. That relationship is found in points (2,8) , (3,12), (4,16), (5,20) etc., |

Lesson 10: Represent Proportions by Equations

Question No.	Answer	Detailed Explanations
1	B	Divide the total cost by the number of hats: $\frac{18}{3} = 6$. This gives the cost per hat, which is the constant of proportionality in the equation: $C = 6n$.
2	A	Choose a pair of data. Divide the value of y by the value of x: $\frac{14}{1} = 14$. This gives the constant of proportionality in the equation: $y = 14x$.
3	D	Divide the total cost by the number of months: $\frac{100}{4} = 25$. This gives the cost per month, which is the constant of proportionality in the equation: $C = 25m$.
4	C	Divide the total cost by the number of pounds: $\frac{4.50}{5} = 0.9$. This gives the cost per pound, which is the constant of proportionality in the equation: $C = 0.9p$.
5	A	Divide the rental cost by the area of the apartment: $\frac{600}{800} = 0.75$. This gives the cost per square foot of area, which is the constant of proportionality in the equation: $C = 0.75a$.
6	B	Divide the total cost by the number of desks: $\frac{7000}{350} = 20$. This gives the cost per desk, which is the constant of proportionality in the equation: $C = 20d$.
7	A	Divide the total number of players by the number of teams: $\frac{180}{12} = 15$. This gives the number of players per team, which is the constant of proportionality in the equation: $p = 15t$.
8	D	The relationship named is that between cost and the number of packs. The number of rolls per pack is irrelevant. The cost per pack is already given as $5 per pack, so this is the constant of proportionality in the equation: $C = 5p$
9	B	Divide the total cost by the number of loads: $\frac{1750}{5} = 350$. This gives the cost per load, which is the constant of proportionality in the equation: $C = 350g$.

Question No.	Answer	Detailed Explanations
10	A	The straight line passes through the origin, so the relationship is proportional. Use the values of a point on the line. Divide the pay by the number of hours: $\dfrac{50}{4} = 12.50$. This gives the pay per hour, which is the constant of proportionality in the equation: $P = 12.50h$.
11	$y=7x$	To solve this problem you need to find the constant of proportionality between x and y. You do this by dividing 9.1 by 1.3 and that equals 7. Therefore, $y = 7x$. Another way of looking at this is finding the unit rate by dividing 9.1 by 1.3. The unit rate is 7 miles per one hour. That translates into the equation $y=7x$.
12	C and F	C and F are the correct options. First you find the unit rate by dividing 3.50 by 7. The unit rate is 0.50. To find the cost of buying x number of apples, you would multiply 0.50 by x.

13

	x = 9	x = 10	x = 7
$\dfrac{x}{15} = \dfrac{3}{5}$	■	☐	☐
$\dfrac{16}{14} = \dfrac{8}{x}$	☐	☐	■
$\dfrac{4}{20} = \dfrac{2}{x}$	☐	■	☐
$\dfrac{75}{x} = \dfrac{50}{6}$	■	☐	☐

To solve for x, you calculate the cross products and solve for x. Therefore, 15 times 3=5x, 75 times 6=50x, 14 times 8 = 16x, and 20 times 2 = 4x. Solve for x by dividing by the coefficient next to x.

Chapter 3
Geometric Reasoning

Lesson 1: Area of Polygons

1. Find the area of a trapezoid with bases of length 8 cm and 12 cm, and a height of 8 cm. Select the correct answer option from the ones given below.

   Ⓐ 60 cm²
   Ⓑ 64 cm²
   Ⓒ 32 cm²
   Ⓓ 128 cm²

2. A trapezoid has bases of length 12 m and 16 m, and its area is 84 m². Find its height.

   Ⓐ 3 meters
   Ⓑ 4 meters
   Ⓒ 6 meters
   Ⓓ 12 meters

3. A trapezoid has an area of 48 cm². If the bases are 5 cm and 9 cm, find its height. Round your answer to two decimal places.

   Ⓐ 2.45 cm
   Ⓑ 4.42 cm
   Ⓒ 6.24 cm
   Ⓓ 3.43 cm

4. Calculate the area of a parallelogram with a base of 12 cm and a height of 6 cm.

   Ⓐ 70 cm².
   Ⓑ 62 cm².
   Ⓒ 72 cm².
   Ⓓ 78 cm².

5. The area of a parallelogram is 135 m², and its base is 15 m. Find its height.

   Ⓐ 8 meters
   Ⓑ 10 meters
   Ⓒ 9 meters
   Ⓓ 6 meters

6. If the area of a parallelogram is 80 inches², and its height is 10 inches, find the length of its base.

    Ⓐ 8 inches
    Ⓑ 18 inches
    Ⓒ 9 inches
    Ⓓ 12 inches

7. A parallelogram has an area of 72 cm² and a base of 12 cm. What is the height of the parallelogram?

    Ⓐ 9 centimeters.
    Ⓑ 6 centimeters.
    Ⓒ 16 centimeters.
    Ⓓ 8 centimeters.

8. Find the area of a rhombus with diagonals measuring 8 cm and 10 cm.

    Ⓐ 30 cm².
    Ⓑ 50 cm².
    Ⓒ 60 cm².
    Ⓓ 40 cm².

9. A rhombus has an area of 45 m², and one diagonal measures 9 m. Find the length of the other diagonal.

    Ⓐ 10 meters.
    Ⓑ 20 meters.
    Ⓒ 15 meters.
    Ⓓ 30 meters.

10. If the area of a rhombus is 64 inches², and one diagonal measures 8 inches, find the length of its other diagonal.

    Ⓐ 14 inches.
    Ⓑ 15 inches.
    Ⓒ 18 inches.
    Ⓓ 16 inches.

CHAPTER 3 → Lesson 2: Finding Area, Volume, & Surface Area

1. **Find the area of the rectangle shown below.**

6.3 cm

4.3 cm

- Ⓐ 10.5 square centimeters
- Ⓑ 24 square centimeters
- Ⓒ 27.09 square centimeters
- Ⓓ 21 square centimeters

2. **What is the volume of a cube whose sides measure 8 inches?**

- Ⓐ 24 in³
- Ⓑ 64 in³
- Ⓒ 128 in³
- Ⓓ 512 in³

3. **Calculate the area of the following polygon.**

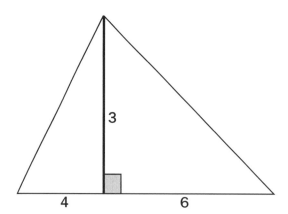

3

4   6

- Ⓐ 15 square units
- Ⓑ 30 square units
- Ⓒ 36 square units
- Ⓓ 18 square units

4. **Calculate the area of the following polygon.**

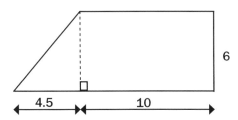

   ⓐ 60 square units
   ⓑ 73.5 square units
   ⓒ 13.5 square units
   ⓓ 24 square units

5. **What is the volume of the following triangular prism?**

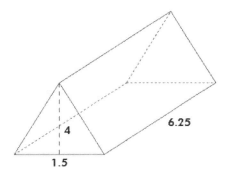

   ⓐ 11.75 cubic units
   ⓑ 20 cubic units
   ⓒ 37.5 cubic units
   ⓓ 18.75 cubic units

6. **What is the volume of a prism with the following base and a height of 2.75?**

   ⓐ 8.25 cubic units
   ⓑ 13.75 cubic units
   ⓒ 16.5 cubic units
   ⓓ 8.75 cubic units

7. **What is the surface area of a cube with sides of length 2?**

    Ⓐ 16 square units
    Ⓑ 8 square units
    Ⓒ 24 square units
    Ⓓ 18 square units

8. **What is the surface area of a rectangular prism with dimensions 2, $\dfrac{1}{2}$, and $\dfrac{1}{4}$?**

    Ⓐ 2

    Ⓑ $\dfrac{13}{4}$

    Ⓒ $\dfrac{9}{4}$

    Ⓓ $\dfrac{3}{2}$

9. **Find the area of the shape below. (Round to the nearest tenth). Use pi = 3.14.**

    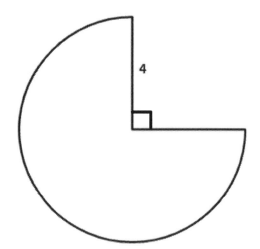

    Ⓐ 37.7 square units
    Ⓑ 50.2 square units
    Ⓒ 18.8 square units
    Ⓓ 35.2 square units

10. John has a container with a volume of 170 cubic feet filled with sand. He wants to transfer his sand into the new container shown below so he can store more sand. After he transfers the sand, how much more sand is remaining in the old container?

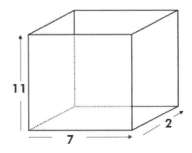

Ⓐ 16 cubic feet of sand
Ⓑ 26 cubic feet of sand
Ⓒ 150 cubic feet of sand
Ⓓ 324 cubic feet of sand

11. What is the area of the shape? Write your answer in the box given below.

56 in.

123 in.

12. Match the question with the correct type of measurement.

	Area	Surface Area	Volume
How much liquid does this bucket hold?	○	○	○
How much wrapping paper do I need to cover or wrap a box?	○	○	○
How much carpet do I need to cover the floor of this room?	○	○	○

13. Find the volume of a right pyramid that has a height of 14 in. and a base area of 25 in². Round your answer to the nearest whole number and write the answer in the box.

14. Match the formula to the correct term.

Area of a triangle

Volume of a cube

Area of rectangle

S^3 $l.w$ $½.l.bh$

15. What is the volume of a rectangular prism with dimensions 6, $\dfrac{1}{2}$, $\dfrac{1}{4}$ feet?

CHAPTER 3 → Lesson 3: Circles

1. **A circle is divided into 4 equal sections. What is the measure of each of the angles formed at the center of the circle?**

   Ⓐ 25°
   Ⓑ 180°
   Ⓒ 90°
   Ⓓ 360°

2. **What is the area of a circle with diameter 8 cm? Round your answer to the nearest tenth. Use π = 3.14.**

   Ⓐ 201.1 cm²
   Ⓑ 201.0 cm²
   Ⓒ 50.2 cm²
   Ⓓ 25.1 cm²

3. **What is the radius of a circle with a circumference of 125 cm? Round your answer to the nearest whole number. Use π = 3.14.**

   Ⓐ 24 cm
   Ⓑ 10 cm
   Ⓒ 20 cm
   Ⓓ 19 cm

4. **What is the circumference of a circle with radius 0.5 feet? Round your answer to the nearest tenth. Use π = 3.14.**

   Ⓐ 3.1 ft
   Ⓑ 3.2 ft
   Ⓒ 0.8 ft
   Ⓓ 0.7 ft

5. **Which of the following could constitute the area of a circle?**

   Ⓐ 50 units
   Ⓑ 1 square unit
   Ⓒ 1.5 cubic units
   Ⓓ One half of a unit

6. If two radii form a 30 degree angle at the center of a circle with radius 10 cm, what is the area between them? Round your answer to the nearest tenth. Use π = 3.14.

   Hint: A circle "sweeps out" 360 degrees.

   Ⓐ 26.2 square centimeters
   Ⓑ 26.1 square centimeters
   Ⓒ 314.1 square centimeters
   Ⓓ 314.2 square centimeters

7. What is the area of a circle with radius 2.8 cm? Round your answer to the nearest tenth. Use π = 3.14.

   Ⓐ 24.7 cm²
   Ⓑ 24.6 cm²
   Ⓒ 17.6 cm²
   Ⓓ 8.8 cm²

8. What is the radius of a circle with area 50 square cm? Round your answer to the nearest whole number. Use π = 3.14.

   Ⓐ 4 cm
   Ⓑ 3 cm
   Ⓒ 8 cm
   Ⓓ 7 cm

9. What is the length of a semi-circle (curved part only) with radius 8 in? Round your answer to the nearest tenth. Use π = 3.14.

   Hint: A semi-circle is half a circle.

   Ⓐ 201.0 in
   Ⓑ 50.2 in
   Ⓒ 100.5 in
   Ⓓ 25.1 in

10. What is the diameter of a circle with an area of 50.24 m²? Use π = 3.14.

   Ⓐ 4 m
   Ⓑ 6 m
   Ⓒ 8 m
   Ⓓ 16 m

11. A circular frisbee has a circumference of 15.2 inches. What is the area of this frisbee?

Use 3.14 for pi. Round to the nearest whole number if needed.

12. Match the description with the correct radius that corresponds with the area or circumference. Use $\pi = 3.14$.

	Radius = 4in.	Radius = 5in.
The circumference of a circle is 31.4 in. Use 3.14 for π.	○	○
The area of a circle is 78.5 in². Use 3.14 for π.	○	○
The area of a circle is 50.24 in². Use 3.14 for π.	○	○
The circumference of a circle is 25.12 in. Use 3.14 for π.	○	○

13. What is the area of a circle with a diameter of 24in.?

Use 3.14 for pi. Round to the nearest whole number if needed.

CHAPTER 3 → Lesson 4: Scale Models

1. **Triangle ABC and triangle PQR are similar. Find the value of x.**

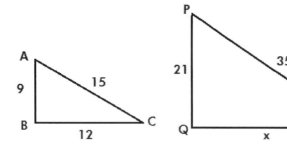

   Ⓐ 23
   Ⓑ 25
   Ⓒ 26
   Ⓓ 28

2. **If the sides of two similar figures have a similarity ratio of $\dfrac{3}{2}$ what is the ratio of their areas?**

   Ⓐ $\dfrac{9}{4}$

   Ⓑ $\dfrac{3}{2}$

   Ⓒ $\dfrac{1}{3}$

   Ⓓ $\dfrac{3}{1}$

LumosLearning.com

3. What is the similarity ratio between the following two similar figures?

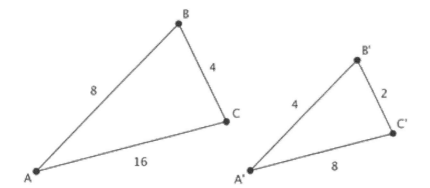

Ⓐ $\dfrac{2}{1}$

Ⓑ $\dfrac{1}{4}$

Ⓒ $\dfrac{2}{3}$

Ⓓ $\dfrac{3}{2}$

4. A map is designed with a scale of 1 inch for every 5 miles. If the distance between two towns is 3 inches on the map, how far apart are they?

Ⓐ 15 miles
Ⓑ 3 miles
Ⓒ 5 miles
Ⓓ 1.5 miles

5. If the angles of one of two similar triangles are 30, 60, and 90 degrees, what are the angles for the other triangle?

Ⓐ 60, 120, 180
Ⓑ 45, 45, 90
Ⓒ 30, 60, 90
Ⓓ There is not enough information to determine.

6. The ratio of similarity between two figures is $\dfrac{4}{3}$.

   If one side of the larger figure is 12 cm long, what is the length of the corresponding side in the smaller figure?

   Ⓐ 9 cm
   Ⓑ 16 cm
   Ⓒ 3 cm

   Ⓓ $\dfrac{4}{3}$ cm

7. If the sides of two similar figures have a similarity ratio of $\dfrac{5}{3}$ what is the ratio of their perimeters?

   Ⓐ $\dfrac{25}{9}$

   Ⓑ $\dfrac{5}{6}$

   Ⓒ $\dfrac{5}{3}$

   Ⓓ $\dfrac{3}{5}$

8. Triangle ABC and triangle DEF are similar. Find the value of x.

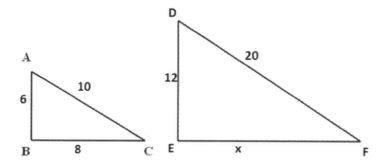

   Ⓐ 16
   Ⓑ 18
   Ⓒ 14
   Ⓓ 12

9. Triangle ABC and triangle DEF are similar. Find the value of x.

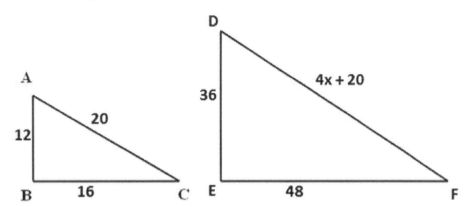

Ⓐ 5
Ⓑ 20
Ⓒ 10
Ⓓ 15

10. Triangle ABC and triangle DEF are similar. Find the value of x.

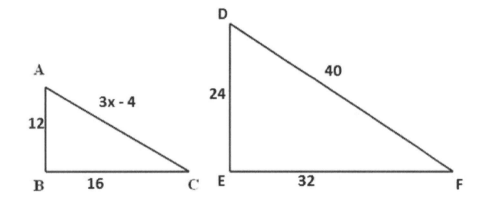

Ⓐ 5
Ⓑ 10
Ⓒ 8
Ⓓ 6

11. On a map, 1 inch equals 15 miles. Two cities are 6 inches apart on the map. What is the actual distance between the cities?

Write your answer in the box given below

12. On a map, 1.5 inches equals 150 miles. The distance that a man travels is 4 inches on the map. Represent the scale as two different ratios.

Note: Select two ratios that represent the scale of the map.

Ⓐ $\frac{150 \text{ miles}}{1.5 \text{ inches}}$

Ⓑ $\frac{1.5 \text{ inches}}{150 \text{ miles}}$

Ⓒ $\frac{4 \text{ inches}}{150 \text{ miles}}$

Ⓓ $\frac{150 \text{ miles}}{4 \text{ inches}}$

13. Mark the map with the correct scale for the situation described.

	Map 1 Scale is 1 in : 15 miles	Map 2 Scale is 2 in : 25 miles
Frank traveled an actual distance of 45 miles. On the map, he traveled 3 inches.	○	○
Two cities are 135 miles apart. On the map, they are 9 inches apart.	○	○
It is 137.5 miles from City 1 to City 2. On the map, City 1 and City 2 are 11 inches apart.	○	○
The map shows that the school and library are 5 inches apart. Therefore they are 62.5 miles apart.	○	○

CHAPTER 3 → Lesson 5: Surface Area of Cylinders

1. **A cylindrical water tank has a height of 10 meters and a diameter of 5 meters. Calculate the total surface area of the tank. (Use π = 3.14)**

   Ⓐ 177.35 square meters.
   Ⓑ 186.35 square meters.
   Ⓒ 225.35 square meters.
   Ⓓ 196.35 square meters.

2. **A cylindrical can of soup has a radius of 4 centimeters and a height of 12 centimeters. Determine the lateral surface area (excluding the top and bottom) of the can. (Use π = 3.14)**

   Ⓐ 401.59 square centimeters.
   Ⓑ 451.6 square centimeters.
   Ⓒ 301.59 square centimeters.
   Ⓓ 331.33 square centimeters.

3. **A pipe has a diameter of 7 inches and a length of 30 inches. Find the surface area of the pipe. (Use π = 3.14)**

   Ⓐ 650.18 square inches.
   Ⓑ 745.18 square inches.
   Ⓒ 666.18 square inches.
   Ⓓ 548.18 square inches.

4. **A cylindrical container with a height of 15 centimeters and a surface area of 330 square centimeters. Calculate the radius of the container. (Use π = 3.14)**

   Ⓐ 3.09 centimeters.
   Ⓑ 23.09 centimeters.
   Ⓒ 12.09 centimeters.
   Ⓓ 2.09 centimeters.

5. **A cardboard tube has a length of 24 inches and a lateral surface area of 150 square inches. Determine the radius of the tube. (Use π = 3.14)**

   Ⓐ 2.98 inches.
   Ⓑ 1.68 inches.
   Ⓒ 0.98 inches.
   Ⓓ 5.5 inches.

6. A cylindrical container has a volume of 1000 cubic centimeters and a height of 20 centimeters. Calculate its radius. (Use π = 3.14)

Ⓐ 5.18 centimeters.
Ⓑ 103.18 centimeters.
Ⓒ 3.18 centimeters.
Ⓓ 4.88 centimeters.

7. A cylindrical pillar has a radius of 8 feet and a lateral surface area of 400 square feet. Calculate the height of the pillar. (Use π = 3.14)

Ⓐ 10.6 feet.
Ⓑ 6.55 feet.
Ⓒ 9.99 feet.
Ⓓ 7.96 feet.

8. A cylindrical pillar has a radius of 8 feet and a lateral surface area of 400 square feet. Calculate the height of the pillar. (Use π = 3.14)

Ⓐ 429.99 square inches.
Ⓑ 399.99 square inches.
Ⓒ 376.99 square inches.
Ⓓ 256.99 square inches.

9. A cylindrical water well has a diameter of 6 meters and a height of 30 meters. Find the total surface area of the well. (Use π = 3.14)

Ⓐ 336.08 square meters.
Ⓑ 277.18 square meters.
Ⓒ 430.08 square meters.
Ⓓ 226.08 square meters.

10. A soda can has a radius of 2.5 centimeters and a lateral surface area of 100 square centimeters. Calculate the height of the can. (Use π = 3.14)

Ⓐ 4.01 centimeters.
Ⓑ 7.11 centimeters.
Ⓒ 5.33 centimeters.
Ⓓ 9.27 centimeters.

CHAPTER 3 → Lesson 6: Volume of Cylinders

1. **Find the volume of a right circular cylinder with a radius of 5 cm and a height of 10 cm. (Use π = 3.14)**

   (A) 350π cm³
   (B) 270π cm³
   (C) 200π cm³
   (D) 250π cm³

2. **A cylindrical water tank has a diameter of 8 meters and a height of 12 meters. Calculate its volume. (Use π = 3.14)**

   (A) 172π m³
   (B) 199π m³
   (C) 192π m³
   (D) 153π m³

3. **A cylindrical container with a radius of 6 inches is filled with oil to a height of 15 inches. Calculate the volume of oil in the container. (Use π = 3.14)**

   (A) 500π in³
   (B) 540π in³
   (C) 440π in³
   (D) 530π in³

4. **The volume of a cylinder is 1000 cubic units, and its height is 20 units. Find the radius of the cylinder. (Use π = 3.14)**

   (A) 3.52 units
   (B) 2.52 units
   (C) 2.11 units
   (D) 5.5 units

5. **A cylindrical water tower has a volume of 1500 m³. If its height is 30 meters, find its radius. (Use π = 3.14)**

   (A) 2.74 meters
   (B) 3.4 meters
   (C) 2.56 meters
   (D) 3.74 meters

6. A cylinder has a radius of 5 cm and a height of 10 cm. Calculate its volume. (Use π = 3.14)

    Ⓐ 250π cm³
    Ⓑ 200π cm³
    Ⓒ 350π cm³
    Ⓓ 450π cm³

7. A cylindrical container has a volume of 500 cubic centimeters. If its height is twice the radius, find the height of the container. (Use π = 3.14)

    Ⓐ 8.97 cm
    Ⓑ 9 cm
    Ⓒ 8.01 cm
    Ⓓ 7.52 cm

8. A cylindrical tank with a radius of 6 meters is filled with water to a height of 9 meters. How much water is in the tank in liters? (1 cubic meter = 1000 liters) (Use π = 3.14)

    Ⓐ 444,000π liters
    Ⓑ 300,000π liters
    Ⓒ 24,000π liters
    Ⓓ 324,000π liters

9. A cylindrical container has a diameter of 10 inches and is filled with sand up to a height of 7 inches. Calculate the volume of sand in the container. (Use π = 3.14)

    Ⓐ 75π in³
    Ⓑ 225π in³
    Ⓒ 175π in³
    Ⓓ 55π in³

10. A cylindrical pencil holder has a volume of 1000 cm³. If its height is 20 cm, find the radius of the pencil holder. (Use π = 3.14)

    Ⓐ 2.82 cm
    Ⓑ 3.8 cm
    Ⓒ 2.03 cm
    Ⓓ 5.82 cm

End of Geometric Reasoning

Chapter 3
Geometric Reasoning

Lesson 1: Area of Polygons

Question No.	Answer	Detailed Explanations
1	B	Area = ½ × (a + b) × h. Substituting the values, Area = ½ × (8 cm + 12 cm) × 8 cm ½ × 20 cm × 8 cm = 80 cm².
2	C	Area = ½ × (a + b) × h. 84 m² = ½ × (12 m + 16 m) × h $h = \dfrac{84 \text{ m}^2}{½} \times (12 \text{ m} + 16 \text{ m})$ $h = \dfrac{84 \text{ m}^2}{14\text{mh}} = 6$ m.
3	D	Area = ½ × (a + b) × h. 48 cm² = (½) × (5 cm + 9 cm) × h $h = \dfrac{48 \text{ cm}^2}{½} \times (5 \text{ cm} + 9 \text{ cm})$ $h = \dfrac{48 \text{ cm}^2}{14\text{cm h}} = 3.43$ cm The height of the trapezoid is 3.43 centimeters.
4	C	Area = base × height. Area = 12 cm × 6 cm = 72 cm².
5	C	Area = base × height 135 m² = 15 m × h $h = \dfrac{135\text{m}^2}{15\text{m}}$ h = 9 m.

Question No.	Answer	Detailed Explanations
6	A	Area = base × height 80 in² = base × 10 in $base = \dfrac{80 \text{ in}^2}{10 \text{ in}}$ base = 8 in.
7	B	Area = base × height 72 cm² = 12 cm × h $h = \dfrac{72 \text{ cm}^2}{12 \text{ cm}}$ h = 6 cm.
8	D	Area = ½ × (d_1 × d_2). Area = ½ × (8 cm × 10 cm) = 40 cm².
9	A	Area = ½ × (d_1 × d_2). 45 m² = ½ × (9 m × d_2) $d_2 = \dfrac{45 \text{ m}^2}{\text{½}} \times 9 \text{ m}$ $d_2 = \dfrac{45 \text{ m}^2}{4.5 \text{ m}}$ d_2 = 10 m.
10	D	Area = ½ × (d_1 × d_2). 64 in² = ½ × (8 in × d_2) $d_2 = \dfrac{64 \text{ in}^2}{\text{½}} \times 8 \text{ in}$ $d_2 = \dfrac{64 \text{ in}^2}{4 \text{in}}$ d_2 = 16 in.

Lesson 2: Finding Area, Volume, & Surface Area

Question No.	Answer	Detailed Explanations
1	C	The answer is 27.09 square centimeters. To calculate the area of a rectangle, multiply the length and width. Multiplying $6.3 \times 4.3 = 27.09$ square centimeters.
2	D	The answer is 512 in³. The formula for the volume for a cube is $V = s^3$, where s is the length of one side. Multiplying $8 \times 8 \times 8 = 512$ in³.
3	A	The correct answer is 15 square units. To find the correct answer, apply the formula for the area of a triangle, $A = \frac{1}{2}bh$. First, calculate the base by adding $6 + 4 = 10$. Next, multiply the base times the height: $10 \times 3 = 30$. Then, divide the product by 2: $30 \div 2 = 15$ square units.
4	B	The answer is 73.5 square units. This is a compound figure comprised of a triangle and a rectangle. Identify the length and width of rectangle. Apply the formula for area of a rectangle, $A = bh$ or $A = lw$, and the formula for the area of a triangle, $A = \frac{1}{2}bh$. Then, add the two products together. The sum is the total area of the figure. (1) area of rectangle: $6 \times 10 = 60$ square units (2) area of triangle : $(\frac{1}{2}) \times 4.5 \times 6 = 13.5$ square units (3) $60 + 13.5 = 73.5$ square units
5	D	The answer is 18.75 cubic units. The formula for volume is $V = BH$, where B = the area of the base, and H = height. Since the base is a triangle, the formula is $V = (\frac{1}{2}bh)(H)$. To solve, plug in the numbers: $V=(\frac{1}{2}bh)(H) =(\frac{1}{2} \times 1.5 \times 4)(6.25) = (3)(6.25) = 18.75$ cubic units.
6	C	The answer is 16.5 cubic units. The formula for volume is $V = BH$, where B = the area of the base, and H = height. Since the base is a parallelogram, the formula is $V = (bh)(H)$. To solve, plug in the numbers: $V=(bh)(H)=(2 \times 3)(2.75)=(6)(2.75)=16.5$ cubic units.
7	C	A cube has 6 square faces. In this particular cube, each face has an area of $2 \times 2 = 4$ square units. The overall surface area $= 6 \times 4 = 24$ square units

Question No.	Answer	Detailed Explanations
8	B	This prism is made up of 6 rectangles. Two of them are 2 by 0.5, two of them are 2 by 0.25, and two of them are 0.5 by 0.25 The surface area = 2(2)(0.5) + 2(2)(0.25) + 2(0.5)(0.25) = 3.25 square units, or $\frac{13}{4}$ square units.
9	A	The answer is 37.7 square units. First, find the area of the entire circle by applying the area formula—πr^2. Next, multiply the area by $\frac{3}{4}$ in order to find the area of the shape. (1) πr^2 (2) 3.14×4^2 = (3) 3.14×16 = (4) Area = 50.24 cm² (5) $50.24 \times \frac{3}{4}$ = 37.68 = (6) 37.68 = 37.7 cm²
10	A	Volume of the new container = l × w × h = 7 x 2 x 11 = 154 cubic feet. Therefore, after transferring the sand, amount of sand remaining in the old container = 170 - 154 = 16 cubic feet.
11	6,888	Use the formula A = L x W

Question 12:

	Area	Surface Area	Volume
How much liquid does this bucket hold?			●
How much wrapping paper do I need to cover or wrap a box?		●	
How much carpet do I need to cover the floor of this room?	●		

Volume is the amount of space occupied by a 3D shape. Area is the amount of space occupied by a 2D shape. Surface area is the area of the surfaces of a 3D shape.

| 13 | 117 | The formula for volume of a right pyramid is $\frac{1}{3}$rd of the product of the height and the base area. Therefore $\frac{1}{3}$(14 x 25) = 116.666... Rounded to the nearest whole number is 117 in³. |

Question No.	Answer	Detailed Explanations
14		

Area of a triangle — $\frac{1}{2} \times b \times h$

Volume of a cube — S^3

Area of rectangle — $l \times b$

(1) Area of a triangle is given by $\frac{1}{2} \times b \times h$. Where b is breadth and h is height

(2) Volume of a cube is given by s^3. Where s is the side

(3) Area of a rectangle is given by $l \times b$. Where l is the length and b is the breadth

Question No.	Answer	Detailed Explanations
15	$\frac{3}{4}$	The volume of a rectangular prism is given by $l.b.h$

Hence, volume $= 6 \times \frac{1}{2} \times \frac{1}{4} = \frac{3}{4}$ ft³

Lesson 3: Circles

Question No.	Answer	Detailed Explanations
1	C	The correct answer is 90°. Selecting 25° results from incorrectly applying the qualities of a circle graph to the circle (a whole circle represents 100%, so four equal parts equal 25% each). Choosing 180° is a result of measuring the angle of the line formed by dividing the circle into two equal parts (a straight line measures 180°). A circle measures 360°, so the measure of each angle formed at the center would be less than 360°. By dividing it into 4 equal pieces, each angle will be 360 ÷ 4 = 90°.
2	C	The correct answer is 50.2 cm². To find the area of a circle, apply the formula $A = \pi r^2$. Since the problem gives the diameter of the circle, the first step is to find the radius by dividing the diameter by 2. 8 ÷ 2 = 4 cm. Next, plug in the numbers into the formula: (1) $\pi 4^2$ = (2) 3.14 x 4^2 = (3) 3.14 x 16 = (4) 50.24 cm² (5) 50.2 cm² (rounded to the nearest tenth). Common errors made when applying the area formula to circles are multiplying the radius by 2 instead of by itself (which would result in 25.1 cm²) or using the diameter of the circle to find the area (resulting in 201.0 cm²).
3	C	The correct answer is 20 cm. To find the radius when given the circumference of the circle, use $\frac{C}{2\pi}$, where C equals circumference. Insert the numbers from the problem, and solve: (1) $r = \frac{C}{2\pi}$ (2) 125 ÷ (2 x 3.14) = (3) 125 ÷ 6.28 = (4) 19.90 cm = (5) 20 cm (rounded to the nearest whole number). Finding a radius of 19 cm results from rounding down instead of rounding up. An answer of 10 cm results from dividing the radius by 2. Choosing 24 cm is based on adding $2 + \pi$ and dividing 125 by the sum.
4	A	The answer is 3.1 ft. Finding 3.2 ft results from rounding up instead of rounding down. A result of 0.8 ft comes from applying the formula for the area of a circle. Selecting 0.7 ft also results from using the area formula but also includes a rounding error. To apply the formula for the circumference of a circle, $2\pi r$, plug in the given values, and solve. (1) $2\pi r$ (2) $2 \times 3.14 \times 0.5$ (3) 6.28×0.5 = (4) 3.14 ft = (5) 3.1 ft (rounded to the nearest tenth).
5	B	The answer is 1 square unit. Area is defined as the number of square units that cover a specific space. Since the question calls for the area of a circle, the best answer is 1 square unit.

Question No.	Answer	Detailed Explanations
6	A	The answer is 26.2 square centimeters. First, find the area of the entire circle by applying the area formula —> $A = \pi r^2$. (1) $A = 3.14 \times 10^2 = 3.14 \times 100 = 314$ cm². Next, calculate the number of square centimeters per degree by dividing the area of the circle by the number of degrees in the circle. (2) $314 \div 360 = 0.87$ cm² per degree. Multiply the quotient by 30 and round to the nearest tenth. (3) $30 \times 0.87 = 26.16$ square centimeters (4) 26.2 cm² (rounded to the nearest tenth).
7	B	The correct answer is 24.6 cm². Area of a circle is given by $A = \pi r^2$, plug in the given values, and solve. $A = 3.14 \times 2.8^2 = 3.14 \times 7.84 = 24.61$ cm². Thus, area of the circle is 24.6 cm² (rounded to the nearest tenth).
8	A	The answer is 4 cm. To apply the formula for finding radius when given area of a circle, which is the square root of A/π, plug in the given values and solve. $r = $ square root of $A/\pi = $ square root of $(50 \div 3.14) = $ square root $(15.92) = 3.99$ cm. Thus, $r = 4$ cm (rounded to the nearest whole number).
9	D	The answer is 25.1 in. To apply the formula for circumference of a circle, $2\pi r$, plug in the given values and solve. Then, divide the circumference by 2 to find the circumference of the semi-circle. Circumference of Circle $= 2\pi r$ $C = 2 \times 3.14 \times 8$ $= 6.28 \times 8 = 50.24$ Circumference of semicircle $= 50.24 \div 2$ $= 25.12$ in $= 25.1$ in (rounded to the nearest tenth) Alternate Method : Perimeter of a semi-circle $= \pi r = 3.14 \times 8 = 25.12 = 25.1$ in (rounded to the nearest tenth).
10	C	An answer of 4 m results from calculating the radius by dividing $50.24 \div 3.14$ and then finding the square root of the quotient, 16. Selecting 6 m results from following the preceding steps, but then adding $4 + 2$. Choosing 16 m is the result of dividing $50.24 \div 3.14$. In order to find the diameter, apply the formula for diameter after finding the radius. The formula is $d = 2r$ (diameter $= 2 \times$ radius). As mentioned, the radius is 4 m. Therefore, $4 \times 2 = 8$ m.

Question No.	Answer	Detailed Explanations
11	18	The formula for area is πr^2 (where r is radius). The formula for circumference is πd (where d is the diameter). If the circumference is 15.2 then if you divide by π, you can find the d. Then d=4.8407. Then the radius r=2.42. Therefore the area is $\pi(2.42)^2$. Therefore the area is 18 in² (rounded to the nearest whole number).

12			Radius = 4 in.	Radius = 5 in.
		The circumference of a circle is 31.4 in. Use 3.14 for π.		●
		The area of a circle is 78.5 in². Use 3.14 for π.		●
		The area of a circle is 50.24 in². Use 3.14 for π.	●	
		The circumference of a circle is 25.12 in. Use 3.14 for π.	●	

Use the formulas for area= πr^2 and circumference= $2\pi r$.

(1) radius = circumference / 2π. radius=31.4 / (2 x 3.14)=31.4/6.28=5 in.
(2) radius = sq. root (area / π). radius=sq. root (78.5/3.14)=sq. root (25)=5 in.
(3) radius = sq. root (area / π). radius=sq. root (50.24/3.14)=sq. root (16)=4in.
(4) radius = circumference / 2π. radius=25.12 / (2 x 3.14)=25.12/6.28=4 in.

Question No.	Answer	Detailed Explanations
13	452	The formula for area is πr^2 (where r is radius). If d=24. Then the radius r=12. Therefore the area is $\pi(12)^2$. Therefore the area is 452 in² (rounded to the nearest whole number).

Lesson 4: Scale Models

Question No.	Answer	Detailed Explanations
1	D	Remember: In order to solve a similarity question, set up a proportion with corresponding sides, and solve!: $\frac{x}{12} = \frac{35}{15}$ or $\frac{x}{12} = \frac{21}{9}$. You can use cross products (ad = bc) to solve for x. (1) $\frac{x}{12} = \frac{35}{15}$ (2) 15x = (35)(12) (3) 15x = 420 (4) x = 420 ÷ 15 (5) x = 28
2	A	If the similarity ratio is $\frac{3}{2}$, then the ratio of the areas is the square of that ratio: $\frac{3}{2} \times \frac{3}{2} = \frac{9}{4}$.
3	A	In order to solve a similarity problem, set up a proportion with corresponding sides: $\frac{8}{4} = \frac{16}{8}$. Both ratios in simplest form are $\frac{2}{1}$. Therefore, the similarity ratio is $\frac{2}{1}$.
4	A	You can use cross products (ad = bc) to solve for x. (inch)/(miles) = (inch)/(miles) (1) $\frac{1}{5} = \frac{3}{x}$ (2) 1x = (3)(5) (3) x = 15 Therefore, the towns are 15 miles apart.
5	C	Corresponding angles are congruent in similar figures. Thus, the angles will have the same measures in the second figure as in the first.
6	A	larger side / smaller side = $\frac{4}{3}$ or larger side = $(\frac{4}{3})$x smaller side. Therefore, smaller side = larger side ÷ $(\frac{4}{3})$. Therefore, in order to find the length of the smaller side, divide 12 by $\frac{4}{3}$. (1) $\frac{12}{1} ÷ \frac{4}{3}$ (2) $\frac{12}{1} \times \frac{4}{3}$ (3) $\frac{12 \times 3}{1 \times 4}$ (4) $\frac{36}{4}$ (5) 9. Therefore, the length of the corresponding side is 9 cm.
7	C	Let the sides of the larger triangle be 5a, 5b and 5c units in length. Then the sides of the smaller triangle will be 3a, 3b and 3c. Therefore the ratio of their perimeters will be $\frac{5(a+b+c)}{3(a+b+c)} = \frac{5}{3}$.

Question No.	Answer	Detailed Explanations
8	A	You can use cross products (ad = bc) to solve for x. (1) $\frac{10}{20} = \frac{8}{x}$ (2) $10x = (20)(8)$ (3) $10x = 160$ (divide both sides by 10) (4) $x = 16$
9	C	You can use cross products (ad = bc) to solve for x. (1) $\frac{16}{48} = \frac{20}{4x + 20}$ (2) $(16)(4x + 20) = (48)(20)$ (3) $64x + 320 = 960$ (subtract both sides by 320) (4) $64x = 640$ (divide each side by 64) (5) $x = 10$
10	C	You can use cross products (ad = bc) to solve for x. (1) $\frac{16}{32} = \frac{3x - 4}{40}$ (2) $(16)(40) = (32)(3x - 4)$ (3) $640 = 96x - 128$ (add both sides by 128) (4) $768 = 96x$ (divide each side by 96) (5) $8 = x$
11	90	15 miles = 1 inch, so 15 x 6 = 90 miles.
12	A and B	A and B are correct options. The scale of the map is a ratio of miles to inches or inches to miles. It does not matter which order you put them in as long as you use the same order when calculating the proportions for distance for the man. You only use the map's information when calculating the scale of the map.

Question No.	Answer	Detailed Explanations

13

	Map 1 Scale is 1 in: 15 miles	Map 2 Scale is 2 in : 25 miles
Frank traveled an actual distance of 45 miles. On the map, he traveled 3 inches.	●	
Two cities are 135 miles apart. On the map, they are 9 inches apart.	●	
It is 137.5 miles from City 1 to City 2. On the map, City 1 and City 2 are 11 inches apart.		●
The map shows that the school and library are 5 inches apart. Therefore they are 62.5 miles apart.		●

Frank traveled an actual distance of 45 miles. On the map, he traveled 3 inches. Therefore, 1 inch on the map corresponds to 45/3 = 15 miles. So, the scale is 1 in : 15 miles.

Two cities are 135 miles apart. On the map, they are 9 inches apart. Therefore, 1 inch on the map corresponds to 135/9 = 15 miles. So, the scale is 1 in : 15 miles.

City 1 and City 2 are 137.5 miles apart. On the map, they are 11 inches apart. Therefore, 1 inch on the map corresponds to 137.5/11 = 12.5 miles. So, the scale is 1 in : 12.5 miles Or 2 in : 25 miles.

The school and library are 62.5 miles apart. Then The map shows that the school and library are 5 inches apart. Therefore, 1 inch on the map corresponds to 62.5/5 = 12.5 miles. So, the scale is 1 in : 12.5 miles Or 2 in : 25 miles.

Lesson 5: Surface Area of Cylinders

Question No.	Answer	Detailed Explanations
1	D	The total surface area of a right circular cylinder is given by the formula A = 2πr(h + r), where r is the radius and h is the height. Plugging in the values, A = 2 × π × 2.5 (10 + 2.5) = 2 × π × 2.5 × 12.5 = 196.35 square meters.
2	C	The lateral surface area of a right circular cylinder is given by the formula A = 2πrh, where r is the radius and h is the height. Plugging in the values, A = 2 × π × 4 × 12 = 301.59 square centimeters (rounded to two places).
3	D	To find the surface area of the pipe, we need to first calculate the radius, which is half of the diameter. The radius is $\frac{7}{2}$ = 3.5 inches. Now, using the formula A = 2πr(h + r), A = 2 × π × 3.5 (30 + 3.5) = 548.18 square inches.
4	D	Given that the surface area (A) is 330 square centimeters and using the formula A = 2πr(h + r), we can rearrange the equation to solve for the radius (r). The formula becomes $r = \sqrt{(\frac{A}{2\pi h})}$. Plugging in the values, $r = \sqrt{(\frac{330}{2 \times \pi \times 15})}$ = 2.09 centimeters.
5	C	The lateral surface area of a cylinder is given by the formula A = 2πrh, where r is the radius and h is the height. We are given A = 150 square inches and h = 24 inches. So, we can rearrange the formula to find the radius $r = \frac{A}{2\pi h}$. Plugging in the values, $r = \frac{150}{2 \times \pi \times 24}$ = 0.98 inches.
6	C	The volume of a right circular cylinder is given by V = πr²h, where r is the radius and h is the height. We are given V = 1000 cubic centimeters and h = 20 centimeters. Rearranging the formula to solve for r, we get $r = \sqrt{(\frac{V}{\pi h})}$. Plugging in the values, $r = \sqrt{(\frac{1000}{\pi \times 20})}$ = 3.18 centimeters.

Question No.	Answer	Detailed Explanations
7	D	The lateral surface area of a cylinder is given by $A = 2\pi rh$, where r is the radius and h is the height. We are given A = 400 square feet and r = 8 feet. Rearranging the formula to solve for h, we get $h = \dfrac{A}{2\pi r}$. Plugging in the values, $h = \left(\dfrac{400}{2 \times \pi \times 20}\right) = 7.96$ feet.
8	C	The total surface area of a cylinder is given by $A = 2\pi r(h + r)$, where r is the radius and h is the height. We are given the diameter, so the radius is $\dfrac{10}{2} = 5$ inches, and h = 14 inches. Plugging in the values, $A = 2 \times \pi \times 5 (14 + 5) = 376.99$ square inches.
9	D	The total surface area of a cylinder is given by $A = 2\pi r(h + r)$, where r is the radius and h is the height. We are given the diameter, so the radius is $\dfrac{6}{2} = 3$ meters, and h = 30 meters. Plugging in the values, $A = 2 \times \pi \times 3 (30 + 3) = 226.08$ square meters.
10	A	The lateral surface area of a cylinder is given by $A = 2\pi rh$, where r is the radius and h is the height. We are given A = 100 square centimeters and r = 2.5 centimeters. Rearranging the formula to solve for h, we get $h = A / (2\pi r)$. Plugging in the values, $h = \dfrac{100}{2 \times \pi \times 2.5} = 4.01$ centimeters.

Lesson 6: Volume of Cylinders

Question No.	Answer	Detailed Explanations
1	D	The formula for the volume of a cylinder is derived from the base area (πr^2) multiplied by the height (h). Substituting the given values gives the volume in terms of π. The formula for the volume of a cylinder is $V = \pi r^2 h$, where r is the radius and h is the height. $V = \pi(5\text{ cm})^2(10\text{ cm}) = 250\pi\text{ cm}^3$
2	C	In this problem, the diameter is given, so we first find the radius ($r = \dfrac{d}{2}$) and then use the formula for the volume of a cylinder. The formula for the volume of a cylinder can also be expressed using diameter (d) instead of radius: $V = \pi(\dfrac{d}{2})^2 h$. $V = \pi(\dfrac{8m}{2})^2(12\text{ m}) = 192\pi\text{ m}^3$
3	B	Given the radius and height, you can directly use the formula for the volume of a cylinder. $V = \pi(6\text{ in})^2(15\text{ in}) = 540\pi\text{ in}^3$
4	B	Rearranging the volume formula to solve for radius, we find the radius given the volume and height. $V = \pi r^2 h$ $1000 = \pi r^2(20)$ $r^2 = \dfrac{1000}{20\pi}$ $r = 2.52$ units
5	A	Rearrange the volume formula to solve for radius. $V = \pi r^2 h$ $1500 = \pi r^2(30)$ $r^2 = \dfrac{1500}{30\pi}$ $r = 2.74$ meters
6	A	Using the formula $V = \pi r^2 h$, with $r = 5$ cm and $h = 10$ cm: $V = \pi \times (5\text{ cm})^2 \times 10\text{ cm} = 250\pi\text{ cm}^3$.
7	A	Set up the equation using the given volume and the relationship between height and radius, then solve for radius and height. Let the radius be r cm. The height is 2r cm. $V = \pi r^2(2r) = 2\pi r^3$ $500 = 2\pi r^3$ $r^3 = \dfrac{500}{2\pi}$ $r \approx 4.48$ cm $h = 2r = 8.97$ cm

Question No.	Answer	Detailed Explanations
8	D	Calculate the volume of water in cubic meters, then convert to liters using the given conversion factor. $V = \pi(6 \text{ m})^2(9 \text{ m}) = 324\pi \text{ m}^3$ Volume in liters $= 324\pi \text{ m}^3 \times 1000 = 324{,}000\pi$ liters
9	C	Calculate the volume using the given diameter and height, while converting to radius. $V = \pi(5 \text{ in})^2(7 \text{ in}) = 175\pi \text{ in}^3$
10	A	Rearrange the volume formula to solve for radius. $V = \pi r^2 h \quad 1000 = \pi r^2(20)$ $r^2 = \dfrac{1000}{20\pi}$ $r = 2.82 \text{ cm}$

Chapter 4
Data Analysis and Probability

Lesson 1: Context of Data Gathered

1. Bella recorded the number of newspapers left over at the end of each day for a week. What is the average number of newspapers left each day?

   3, 6, 1, 0, 2, 3, 6

   Ⓐ 2 newspapers
   Ⓑ 3 newspapers
   Ⓒ 4.3 newspapers
   Ⓓ 6 newspapers

2. Recorded below are the ages of eight friends. Which statement is true about this data set?

   13, 18, 14, 12, 15, 19, 11, 15

   Ⓐ Mean > Median > Mode
   Ⓑ Mode < Mean < Median
   Ⓒ Median > Mode < Median
   Ⓓ Mode > Mean > Median

3. The line plot below represents the high temperature in °F each day of a rafting trip. What was the average high temperature during the trip?

   Ⓐ 70°F
   Ⓑ 71°F
   Ⓒ 71.4°F
   Ⓓ 72°F

4. What is the mean absolute deviation of the grades Charlene received on her first ten quizzes: 83%, 92%, 76%, 87%, 89%, 96%, 88%, 91%, 79%, 99%.

   Ⓐ 4.5%
   Ⓑ 5.4%
   Ⓒ 88%
   Ⓓ 88.5%

5. The following numbers are the minutes it took Nyak to complete one lap around a certain dirt bike course. What is the mean absolute deviation of this data set?

$$12.3, 12.6, 12.2, 10.9, 11.3, 10.3, 11.7, 10.7$$

   Ⓐ 0.7 minutes
   Ⓑ 0.75 minutes
   Ⓒ 11.1 minutes
   Ⓓ 1.5 minutes

6. The local Akita Rescue Organization has nine Akitas for adoption. Their weights are 82 lb, 95 lb, 130 lb, 112 lb, 122 lb, 72 lb, 86 lb, 145 lb, 93 lb. What are the median (M), 1st Quartile (Q1), 3rd Quartile (Q3) and Interquartile Range (IQR) of this data set?

   Ⓐ M = 95, Q1 = 84, Q3 = 126, IQR = 42
   Ⓑ M = 95, Q1 = 85, Q3 = 126, IQR = 145
   Ⓒ M = 95, Q1 = 84, Q3 = 145, IQR = 42
   Ⓓ M = 95, Q1 = 126, Q3 = 145, IQR = 42

7. Monica is keeping track of how much money she spends on lunch each school day. This week Monica spent $5.20, $6.50, $3.75, $0.75, and $4.15. What is the median (M) and Interquartile Range (IQR) of Monica's lunch expense?

   Ⓐ M = $4.15, IQR = $1.45
   Ⓑ M = $4.07, IQR = $1.45
   Ⓒ M = $4.07, IQR = $2.25
   Ⓓ M = $4.15, IQR = $3.60

8. Monica's friend Anna is also tracking her school lunch expenses. This week Anna spent $2.60, $0, $7.00, $4.40, $3.75. What is the difference between Monica's and Anna's average daily lunch expense?

Monica: $5.20, $6.50, $3.75, $0.75, and $4.15

   Ⓐ $0.40
   Ⓑ $0.52
   Ⓒ $0.60
   Ⓓ $1.50

9. Zahra and Tyland are very competitive. Each have recorded their basketball scores since the beginning of the season. Which data set has a greater Interquartile Range (IQR)?

Name	Scores
Zahra	8, 10, 3, 12, 14, 11
Tyland	6, 7, 18, 12, 4, 9

Ⓐ Zahra has the higher IQR of 4.
Ⓑ Zahra has the higher IQR of 10.5.
Ⓒ Tyland's IQR is 2 points higher than Zahra's.
Ⓓ Tyland and Zahra have the same IQR of 5.

10. Jamila records the number of customers she gets each day for a week: 20, 42, 15, 23, 53, 62, 58. What is the mean absolute deviation of this data?

Ⓐ 16.9 customers
Ⓑ 19 customers
Ⓒ 39 customers
Ⓓ 47.5 customers

11. Frank played 9 basketball games this season. His scores were 15, 20, 14, 36, 20, 10, 35, 23, and 24. What is the median of Frank's scores? Write the answer in the box.

12. Gordan has the following data: 13, 19, 16, z, 17
If the mean is 16, which number could be z? Circle the correct answer.

Ⓐ 11
Ⓑ 15
Ⓒ 18

CHAPTER 4 → Lesson 2: Relating Data Distributions

1. **The histogram below shows the grades in Mr. Didonato's history class.**

Which of the following statements is true based on this data?

Ⓐ The mode score is 75%.
Ⓑ More than half the students received 81% or higher.
Ⓒ Ten students received a 70% or lower.
Ⓓ There is not enough information to determine the median score.

2. **The bar graph below shows the different types of shoes sold by *Active Feet*.**

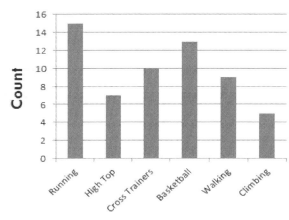

Which of the following statements is true based on this data?

Ⓐ The store carries more types of basketball and climbing shoes combined than types of running shoes.
Ⓑ The store sells more running shoes than any other shoe type.
Ⓒ The store has more types of walking shoes than cross trainers.
Ⓓ The store earns more money selling basketball shoes than walking shoes.

3. Milo and Jacque went fishing and recorded the weight of their fish in the line plots below.

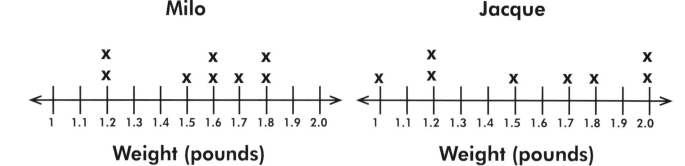

Which of the following statements is true based on this data?

Ⓐ The weights of Milo's fish have more variability.
Ⓑ The average weight of Jacque's fish is greater than the average weight of Milo's fish.
Ⓒ The weights of Jacque's fish have a greater mean absolute deviation.
Ⓓ Milo caught more fish by weight than Jacque.

4. The frequency table below records the age of the student who attended the dance.

Age	Frequency
11	17
12	20
13	9
14	8
15	12
16	4

Which of the following statements is true based on this data?

Ⓐ 80 students attended the dance.
Ⓑ The mean age is 12.86
Ⓒ If 3 more 16-year-olds arrive, the median age would increase.
Ⓓ More than half the students are older than the mean.

5. For twelve weeks Jeb has recorded his car's fuel mileage in miles per gallon (mpg). He has plotted these fuel mileages below in a box plot.

Which of the following statements is true based on this data?

Ⓐ The best fuel mileage recorded was 34 mpg.
Ⓑ Half of the data collected was between 27 mpg and 34 mpg.
Ⓒ The median fuel mileage was 30.5 mpg.
Ⓓ Three data points lie in the Interquartile range.

6. *"Forever Green"* recorded the heights of the pine trees sold this month in the box plot shown below. There are 15 data points in Quartile 3.

Which of the following statements is true based on this data?

Ⓐ About 25% of the trees were 7 feet 3 inches or taller.
Ⓑ There are more data points in Quartile 2 than Quartile 3.
Ⓒ The median height is 6 feet 2 inches.
Ⓓ "Forever Green" sold a total of about 60 trees this month.

7. As part of a math project, each student in Ms. Lauzon's class recorded the number of jumping jacks they could perform in 30 seconds.

Stem	Leaf
3	0 0 2 4 7 7
4	1 1 4 7 9
5	2 3 4 4 6 6 7
6	0 0 1 1 3 8 8
7	1 2
3|0 means 30	

Which of the following statements is true based on this data?

Ⓐ There are 21 students in Ms. Lauzon's class.
Ⓑ The median number of jumping jacks performed was 53.
Ⓒ The range of jumping jacks is 42.
Ⓓ Seven people performed less than 40 jumping jacks.

8. **Tamryn and Clio both make beaded necklaces. The line plots below display the number of beads on ten necklaces each from Tamryn and Clio.**

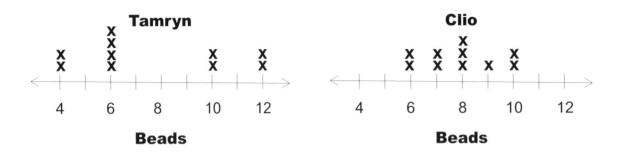

Which of the following statements is true based on this data?

Ⓐ If Tamryn added an eleventh data point of 10, the mean would not change.
Ⓑ On an average, Tamryn uses more beads than Clio.
Ⓒ Clio has more variability in the number of beads she uses.
Ⓓ If Clio added an eleventh data point of 8, the median would stay the same.

9. **The histogram below shows the high temperature each day for a month.**

Which of the following statements is true based on this data?

Ⓐ More than half the days had a temperature of 70−74°.
Ⓑ 20% of the days had temperatures above 74°.
Ⓒ The average temperature was 72°.
Ⓓ There were fewer days below 70° than days above 74°.

10. Marcel enjoys catching fireflies. The steam-and-leaf plot shows the number of fireflies Marcel caught on several nights.

Stem	Leaf
0	4 6 9
1	0 3 4 7 7 7 8
2	0 0 2 2 5
3	1 4
1|3 means 13	

Which of the following statements is true based on this data?

Ⓐ The median is greater than the mean.
Ⓑ The median number of fireflies caught was 17.
Ⓒ The range of fireflies is 34.
Ⓓ Marcel caught fireflies on 14 nights.

11. The students in one math class were asked how many brothers and sisters (siblings) they each have. The plot below shows the distribution of the data (answers from the students). Circle the blue box that represents the number of siblings had by the most students in this class.

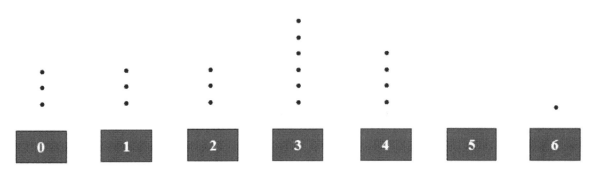

12. Three volleyball teams each recorded their scores for their first 5 games. Use each team's scores below to determine the missing value.

	10	14	17
Team 1: 15, 16, t, 17, 12, Mode = 17, What is t?	○	○	○
Team 2: 7, 14, r, 16, 13 Mean = 12, What is r?	○	○	○
Team 3: 11, 7, 19, 14, z, Median = 14, What is z?	○	○	○

CHAPTER 4 → Lesson 3: Mean, Median, and Mean Absolute Deviation

1. **Consider the following dot-plot for Height versus Weight.**

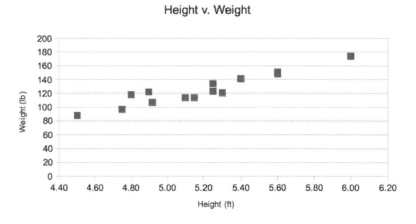

Height v. Weight

What does this dot-plot indicate about the correlation between height and weight?

Ⓐ There is no correlation.
Ⓑ There is a strong negative correlation.
Ⓒ There is a strong positive correlation.
Ⓓ There is a weak positive correlation.

2. **The following chart represents the heights of boys on the basketball and soccer teams.**

Basketball	Soccer
5'4''	4'11''
5'2''	4'10''
5'3''	5'9''
5'5''	5'1''
5'5''	5'0''
5'1''	5'1''
5'9''	5'3''
5'3''	5'1''

What inference can be made based on this information?

Ⓐ Soccer players have a higher average skill level than basketball players.
Ⓑ Soccer players have a lower average weight than basketball players.
Ⓒ Basketball players have a higher average height than soccer players.
Ⓓ No inference can be made.

3. **Use the table below to answer the question that follows:**

Month	Avg Temp.
January	24°F
February	36°F
March	55°F
April	65°F
May	72°F
June	78°F

What is the difference between the mean temperature of the first four months of the year and the mean temperature of the next two months?

Ⓐ 15 degrees
Ⓑ 20 degrees
Ⓒ 25 degrees
Ⓓ 30 degrees

4. **Use the table below to answer the question:**

Month	Avg Temp.
January	24°F
February	36°F
March	55°F
April	65°F
May	72°F
June	78°F

If the temperature in January was 54°F instead of 24°F, by how much would the mean temperature for the six months increase?

Ⓐ 5°F
Ⓑ 10°F
Ⓒ 30°F
Ⓓ 35°F

5. **Use the table to answer the question below:**

Team	Wins
Mustangs	14
Spartans	17
North Stars	16
Hornets	9
Stallions	13
Renegades	9
Rangers	5

What is the mode of the wins for all the teams in the above table?

Ⓐ 14
Ⓑ 5
Ⓒ 13
Ⓓ 9

6. **Jack scored 7, 9, 2, 6, 15 and 15 points in 6 basketball games. Find the mean, median and mode scores for all the games.**

Ⓐ Mean = 7, Median = 9 and Mode = 2
Ⓑ Mean = 9, Median = 7 and Mode = 15
Ⓒ Mean = 9, Median = 8 and Mode = 15
Ⓓ Mean = 7, Median = 2 and Mode = 9

7. **Mean absolute deviation is a measure of...**

Ⓐ Central Tendency
Ⓑ Variability
Ⓒ Averages
Ⓓ Sample Size

8. Calculate the mean for the following set of data:

$$\left\{ \frac{7}{4}, \frac{3}{4}, \frac{5}{4}, \frac{7}{4}, \frac{3}{4}, \frac{5}{4} \right\}$$

Ⓐ $\dfrac{7}{4}$

Ⓑ $\dfrac{5}{2}$

Ⓒ $\dfrac{5}{4}$

Ⓓ $\dfrac{1}{6}$

9. Another word for mean is...

Ⓐ Average
Ⓑ Middle
Ⓒ Most
Ⓓ Count

10. What is the median for the following set of data?

$$\left\{ \frac{4}{5}, \frac{1}{3}, \frac{1}{3}, \frac{1}{5}, \frac{2}{3} \right\}$$

Ⓐ $\dfrac{1}{3}$

Ⓑ $\dfrac{2}{3}$

Ⓒ $\dfrac{1}{5}$

Ⓓ $\dfrac{1}{4}$

11. What is the mode of the following set of data?

{1, 1, 2, 3, 1, 4, 6, 2, 3}

Ⓐ 2
Ⓑ 3.75
Ⓒ 1
Ⓓ 6

12. John scored 6, 8, 1, 5, 11, 14 and 14 points in 7 lacrosse games. Find the mean, median and mode scores for all the games. (Round to the nearest tenth)

Ⓐ Mean = 8.4, Median = 8 and Mode = 14
Ⓑ Mean = 8.1, Median = 6, and Mode = 14
Ⓒ Mean = 9.3, Median = 8 and Mode = 15
Ⓓ Mean = 7.5, Median = 2 and Mode = 9

13. Calculate the mean for the following set of data:

{ 0.3, 1.2, 2.5, 4.3 }

Round your answer to the nearest tenth.

Ⓐ 2.1
Ⓑ 2.7
Ⓒ 8.3
Ⓓ 2.5

14. Calculate the median for the following set of data:

{ 0.3, 1.2, 2.5, 4.3 }

Round your answer to the nearest tenth.

Ⓐ 1.8
Ⓑ 2.1
Ⓒ 1.9
Ⓓ 1.2

15. What is the mean absolute deviation for the following set of data?

{2, 5, 7, 1, 2}

Ⓐ 3.4
Ⓑ 2
Ⓒ 2.08
Ⓓ 5

16. Fill in the blanks in the table with the correct value of mean or median. Round the number to the tenth place in case the answer is not a whole number.

	Median	Mean
Data Set : 9, 8, 7, 4, 5		6.6
Data Set : 5, 8, 5, 9, 1, 2	5	
Data Set : 1, 2, 8, 1, 3, 3		3

17. The mean of a data set is 5. The minimum of the data is 2. What is the deviation of the minimum?

Write your answer in the box given below.

CHAPTER 4 → Lesson 4: Mean, Median, and Mode

1. The following data set represents a score from 1-10 for a customers' experience at a local restaurant.

    { 1, 1, 2, 1, 3, 4, 7, 8, 1, 3, 4, 2, 1, 3, 7, 2 }

    If a score of 1 means the customer did not have a good experience, and a 10 means the customer had a fantastic experience, what can you infer by looking at the data?

    (A) Overall, customers had a good experience.
    (B) Overall, customers had a bad experience.
    (C) Overall, customers had an "ok" experience.
    (D) Nothing can be inferred from this data.

2. The manager of a local pizza place has asked you to make suggestions on how to improve his menu. The following bar graph represents the results of a survey asking customers what their favorite food at the restaurant was.

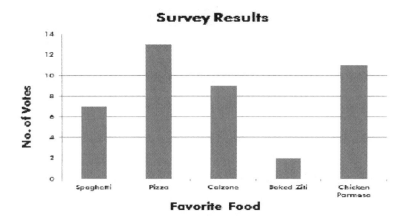

    Based on these survey results, which menu item would you suggest the manager remove from the menu?

    (A) Spaghetti
    (B) Pizza
    (C) Calzone
    (D) Baked Ziti

3. What are the measures of central tendency?

    (A) Mean, Median, Mode
    (B) Median, Mode, Mean Absolute Deviation
    (C) Median, Mean Absolute Deviation, Sample Size
    (D) Mean, Median, Range

4. What is the mean absolute deviation for the following set of data?

{1, 2, 3, 4}

Ⓐ 1
Ⓑ 2.5
Ⓒ 4
Ⓓ 2

5. What are the central tendencies of the following data set? (round to the nearest tenth)

{2, 2, 3, 4, 6, 8, 9, 10, 13, 13, 16, 17}

Ⓐ Mean: 8.6, Median: 8.5, Mode: 2, 13
Ⓑ Mean: 8.5, Median: 8.4, Mode: 2, 3
Ⓒ Mean: 8.5, Median: 8.6, Mode: 2, 13
Ⓓ Mean: 7.6, Median: 7.5, Mode: 10, 13

6. What are the central tendencies of the following data set? (round to the nearest tenth)

{11, 11, 12, 13, 15, 17, 18, 20, 23, 23, 26, 27}

Ⓐ Mean: 17.2, Median: 17.5, Mode: none
Ⓑ Mean: 18.5, Median: 16, Mode: 11
Ⓒ Mean: 17.5, Median: 18, Mode: 23
Ⓓ Mean: 18, Median: 17.5, Mode: 11, 23

7. What are the central tendencies of the following data set? (round to the nearest tenth)

{31, 31, 32, 33, 35, 37, 38, 41, 54, 54, 57, 58}

Ⓐ Mean: 41.4, Median: 37.5, Mode: 31
Ⓑ Mean: 41.5, Median: 36.5, Mode: none
Ⓒ Mean: 41.6, Median: 38.5, Mode: 31, 54
Ⓓ Mean: 41.8, Median: 37.5, Mode: 31, 54

8. What are the central tendencies of the following data set? (round to the nearest tenth)

{41, 41, 42, 43, 45, 47, 48, 51, 64, 64, 64, 67}

Ⓐ Mean: 51.4, Median: 47.5, Mode: 64
Ⓑ Mean: 48.5, Median: 46, Mode: 64
Ⓒ Mean: 47.5, Median: 48, Mode: 64
Ⓓ Mean: 47, Median: 47.5, Mode: 64

9. **What are the central tendencies of the following data set? (round to the nearest tenth)**

   {51, 51, 52, 53, 55, 57, 58, 61, 54, 54, 57, 54}

   Ⓐ Mean: 58.5, Median: 56, Mode: 54
   Ⓑ Mean: 54.8, Median: 54, Mode: 54
   Ⓒ Mean: 57.5, Median: 58, Mode: 54
   Ⓓ Mean: 57.6, Median: 57.5, Mode: 54

10. **What are the central tendencies of the following data set? (round to the nearest tenth)**

   {61, 61, 52, 53, 65, 67, 58, 61, 64, 64, 57, 54}

   Ⓐ Mean: 59.8, Median: 61, Mode: 61
   Ⓑ Mean: 58.5, Median: 66, Mode: 64
   Ⓒ Mean: 57.5, Median: 68, Mode: 64
   Ⓓ Mean: 57.9, Median: 67.5, Mode: 64

11. **What are the central tendencies of the following data set? (round to the nearest tenth)**

   {71, 71, 62, 63, 75, 77, 68, 71, 74, 74, 67, 74}

   Ⓐ Mean: 70.6, Median: 78, Mode: 74
   Ⓑ Mean: 68.5, Median: 76, Mode: 74
   Ⓒ Mean: 70.6, Median: 71, Mode: 71, 74
   Ⓓ Mean: 77, Median: 77.5, Mode: 74

12. **What are the central tendencies of the following data set? (round to the nearest tenth)**

   {61, 71, 52, 63, 65, 77, 58, 71, 64, 74, 57, 74}

   Ⓐ Mean: 65.6, Median: 64.5, Mode: 71, 74
   Ⓑ Mean: 68.5, Median: 66, Mode: none
   Ⓒ Mean: 67.5, Median: 68, Mode: 71
   Ⓓ Mean: 67, Median: 67.5, Mode: 2

13. **What are the central tendencies of the following data set? (round to the nearest tenth)**

   {21, 21, 22, 23, 35, 37, 38, 41, 44, 44, 47, 44}

   Ⓐ Mean: 38.5, Median: 37.5, Mode: 44
   Ⓑ Mean: 34.8, Median: 37.5, Mode: 44
   Ⓒ Mean: 37.5, Median: 38, Mode: none
   Ⓓ Mean: 37, Median: 37.5, Mode: 54

14. Kelli's Ice Cream Shop must have a mean of 110 visitors per day in order to make a profit. The table below shows the number of visitors during one week.

	No of Visitors
Sunday	63
Monday	77
Tuesday	121
Wednesday	96
Thursday	137
Friday	154

Based on the table, how many visitors will need to go to Kelli's Ice Cream shop on Saturday in order for the company to make a profit for the week?

Ⓐ 108
Ⓑ 110
Ⓒ 122
Ⓓ 222

15. Henry made a list of his math scores for one grading period: 98, 87, 93, 89, 90, 85, 88. If Henry adds a 90 to the list to represent his final test for the grading period, which statement is true?

Ⓐ The mode would decrease.
Ⓑ The mean would increase.
Ⓒ The median would increase.
Ⓓ The mean would decrease.

16. Calculate the Mean, Median and Mode for the data set given below.

5, 5, 9, 4, 6, 7

Match the value of the answer to it's correct category.

	Mean	Median	Mode
6	○	○	○
5.5	○	○	○
5	○	○	○

17. Find the interquartile range of the data set.

32.6, 98.5, 16.6, 22.4, 99.8, 72.6, 68.2, 51.8, and 49.3.

CHAPTER 4 → Lesson 5: Sampling a Population

1. **Joe and Mary want to calculate the average height of students in their school. Which of the following groups of students would produce the least amount of bias?**

   Ⓐ Every student in the 8th grade.
   Ⓑ Every student on the school basketball team.
   Ⓒ A randomly selected group of students in the halls.
   Ⓓ Joe & Mary's friends.

2. **Which of the following represents who you should survey in a population?**

   Ⓐ A random, representative group from the population
   Ⓑ Every individual in a population
   Ⓒ Only those in the population that agree with you
   Ⓓ Anyone, including those not in the population

3. **What does increasing the sample size of a survey do for the overall results?**

   Ⓐ Decreases bias in the results
   Ⓑ Increases the mean of the results
   Ⓒ Increases the reliability of the results
   Ⓓ Increasing sample size does not impact the results of a survey

4. **Which of the following is not a valid reason for not surveying everyone in a population?**

   Ⓐ It takes a far longer amount of time to survey everyone.
   Ⓑ Not everyone will be willing to participate in the survey.
   Ⓒ It is hard to determine the exact size of a population necessary to ensure everyone is surveyed.
   Ⓓ Surveying everyone produces unreliable results.

5. **Why is it important to know the sample size of a given survey?**

   Ⓐ It helps determine whether any bias exists.
   Ⓑ It helps determine how reliable the results are.
   Ⓒ It gives a good estimate for the size of the target population.
   Ⓓ It is not important to know the sample size.

6. John and Maggie want to calculate the average height of students in their school. Which of the following groups of students would most likely produce the most amount of bias?

   Ⓐ Every student in the 8th grade.
   Ⓑ Every student on the school basketball team.
   Ⓒ A randomly selected group of students in the halls.
   Ⓓ John & Maggie's friends.

7. Which of the following question types will provide the most useful statistical results?

   Ⓐ Open-ended questions where the person surveyed can answer in any way they want
   Ⓑ Multiple choice questions offering the person a representative number of choices
   Ⓒ True or false questions

8. Which of the following does not represent a way of avoiding bias in survey results?

   Ⓐ Use neutral words in the questions asked
   Ⓑ Ensure a random sample of the population
   Ⓒ Only survey individuals that will answer a certain way
   Ⓓ Tailor the conclusions based on survey results, not previous thoughts

9. The following data set represents survey results on a scale of 1 to 10.

   {8, 8, 9, 8, 6, 7, 7, 7, 8, 8, 6}

   Which of the following survey result would you be most surprised with if given by the next person surveyed?

   Ⓐ 6
   Ⓑ 5
   Ⓒ 8
   Ⓓ 7

10. The following data set represents survey results on a scale of 1 to 10.

    {6, 6, 7, 6, 8, 7, 7, 7, 6, 6, 8}

    Which of the following survey results would you be most surprised with if given by the next person surveyed?

    Ⓐ 6
    Ⓑ 10
    Ⓒ 8
    Ⓓ 7

11. A company is conducting a survey on their performance with customer service. What method will best avoid receiving biased data?

    Ⓐ The company should make the survey anonymous.

    Ⓑ The company should take a video survey.

    Ⓒ The company should require the survey during the transaction.

    Ⓓ The company should just request that everyone fill out a survey.

12. A company is conducting a survey on their performance with customer service. What should the survey look like?

    Ⓐ The survey should contain a few simple multiple choice questions with an optional comment section.

    Ⓑ The survey should contain simple free response questions with an optional comment section. The survey should contain only free response questions.

    Ⓒ The survey should contain some personal questions.

    Ⓓ

13. Where should a survey about personal items purchased be conducted?

    Ⓐ The receipt should have a link to the survey website.

    Ⓑ The survey should be near the register.

    Ⓒ The survey should be near the exit doors.

    Ⓓ The survey should be in the parking lot.

14. How should online video game surveys be conducted?

    Ⓐ This survey should be put at the end of a level or section of the game.

    Ⓑ This survey should be put at the beginning of the game.

    Ⓒ Thus survey should be put on flyers and distributed at a gaming store.

    Ⓓ This survey should be put on the website separate from the game.

15. A large corporation is launching a new product, Hitz, which allows customers to purchase music and store it on the corporation's servers. They want to survey people who listen to a lot of music. Which of the following would give them the best sample?

    Ⓐ Conducting a survey inside of a music store

    Ⓑ Conducting a survey at the parking lot of a music concert

    Ⓒ Conducting an online survey on music social networking websites

    Ⓓ Conducting a survey of students in a school marching band.

16. Match the situation with the sampling method used.

	Convenience Sample	Systematic Sample	Simple Random Sample
A person chooses every 5th person on a list of names starting with #1.	○	○	○
A person accepts the first 15 people to respond to a magazine ad.	○	○	○
A person picks names out of a hat.	○	○	○

17. A jar of marbles contains gray and black marbles. You collect the representative sample shown here:

If the jar contains 50 marbles, about how many marbles are gray?

Write your answer in the box given below.

CHAPTER 4 → Lesson 6: Describing Multiple Samples

1. John comes up with the following methods for generating unbiased samples from shoppers at a mall.

    I. Ask random strangers in the mall

    II. Always go to the mall at the same time of day

    III. Go to different places in the mall

    IV. Don't ask questions the same way to different people

    Which of these techniques represents the best way of generating an unbiased sample?

    Ⓐ   I and II
    Ⓑ   I and III
    Ⓒ   I, II, and III
    Ⓓ   All of these

2. These two samples are about students' favorite subjects. What inference can you make concerning the students' favorite subjects?

Student samples	Science	Math	English Language Arts	Total
#1	40	14	30	84
#2	43	17	33	93

    Ⓐ   Students prefer Science over the other subjects.
    Ⓑ   Students prefer Math over the other subjects.
    Ⓒ   Students prefer English language arts over the other subjects.
    Ⓓ   Students prefer History over the other subjects.

3. These two samples are about students' favorite types of movies. What inference can you make concerning the students' favorite types of movies?

Student samples	Comedy	Action	Drama	Total
#1	35	45	19	99
#2	38	48	22	108

    Ⓐ   Students prefer action movies over the other types.
    Ⓑ   Students prefer drama over the other types.
    Ⓒ   Students prefer comedy over the other types.
    Ⓓ   none

4. **These two samples are about students' favorite fruits. What inference can you make concerning the students' favorite fruits?**

Student samples	Blueberries	Bananas	Strawberries	Total
#1	33	18	44	95
#2	30	20	40	90

- Ⓐ Students prefer strawberries over the other fruits.
- Ⓑ Students prefer bananas over the other fruits.
- Ⓒ Students prefer blueberries over the other fruits.
- Ⓓ none

5. **Jane and Matt conducted two surveys about students' favorite sports to play. What inference can you make concerning the students' favorite sports?**

Student samples	Soccer	Basketball	Tennis	Total
#1	50	145	26	221
#2	56	150	20	226

- Ⓐ Most students like basketball over soccer or tennis.
- Ⓑ Most students like soccer over basketball or tennis.
- Ⓒ Most students like tennis over soccer or basketball.
- Ⓓ Most students like track.

6. **Paul and Maggie conducted two surveys about students' favorite seasons. What inference can you make concerning the students' favorite seasons?**

Student samples	Summer	Fall	Spring	Total
#1	100	128	244	472
#2	98	129	250	477

- Ⓐ Most students prefer the Spring season over Summer and Fall.
- Ⓑ Students prefer the Summer season.
- Ⓒ Students prefer the Fall season.
- Ⓓ Students prefer the Winter season.

7. John and Mark conducted two surveys about students' favorite pizza toppings. What inference can you make concerning the students' favorite pizza toppings?

Student samples	pineapple	pepperoni	extra cheese	Total
#1	145	237	118	500
#2	150	230	120	500

Ⓐ Most students like pepperoni.
Ⓑ Most students like extra cheese.
Ⓒ Most students like pineapple.
Ⓓ The students like pepperoni over pineapple or extra cheese.

8. Jon and Minny conducted two surveys about students' favorite board games. What inference can you make concerning the students' favorite board games?

Student samples	Game X	Game Y	Game Z	Total
#1	45	5	6	56
#2	50	6	2	58

Ⓐ Most students like Game Z.
Ⓑ Most students like **Game X** over **Game Y** or Game Z.
Ⓒ Most students like **Game Y**.
Ⓓ Most students don't like **Game X**.

9. Tom and Bob conducted two surveys about their co-workers' favorite hobbies. What inference can you make concerning their co-workers' favorite hobbies?

Co-worker sample	Play Golf	Play Video Games	Fishing	Total
#1	125	80	126	331
#2	118	83	130	331

Ⓐ Most of their coworkers spend a lot of money.
Ⓑ Most of their coworkers spend a lot of time inside.
Ⓒ Most of their coworkers spend a lot of time outside.
Ⓓ Most of their coworkers live in big houses.

10. **Bill and Jill conducted two surveys about students' favorite card games. What inference can you make concerning the students' favorite card games?**

Student samples	Hearts	Go fish	Spades	Total
#1	14	90	11	115
#2	10	88	14	122

- Ⓐ Most students like speed.
- Ⓑ Most students like hearts.
- Ⓒ Most students like spades.
- Ⓓ Most students like Go fish over hearts or spades.

11. **Moe and Lonnie conducted two surveys about students' favorite soda flavor. What inference can you make concerning the students' favorite soda flavor?**

Student samples	Strawberry	Orange	Rootbeer	Total
#1	10	11	88	109
#2	14	14	90	118

- Ⓐ Most students like strawberry.
- Ⓑ Most students like orange.
- Ⓒ Most students like rootbeer over strawberry or orange.
- Ⓓ Most students like chocolate.

12. **Billy and Larry conducted two surveys about students' favorite subject. What inference can you make concerning the students' favorite subject?**

Student samples	Math	English Language Arts	Science	Total
#1	111	111	111	333
#2	114	114	114	342

- Ⓐ Most students like science.
- Ⓑ Most students like math.
- Ⓒ The same number of students like the three subjects equally.
- Ⓓ Most students like English Language Arts.

13. Tom and Jerry conducted two surveys about students' favorite ice cream flavor. What inference can you make concerning the students' favorite ice cream flavor?

Student samples	Chocolate	Strawberry	Cookies-n-Cream	Total
#1	59	3	12	74
#2	61	4	15	80

Ⓐ Most students' like cookies-n-cream.
Ⓑ Most students like chocolate over strawberry or cookies-n-cream.
Ⓒ Most students' like strawberry.
Ⓓ Most students' like strawberry and cookies-n-cream.

14. Paul and Maggie conducted two surveys about students' favorite holiday. What inference can you make concerning the students' favorite holiday?

Student samples	Christmas	Thanksgiving	Easter	Total
#1	100	128	244	472
#2	98	129	250	477

Ⓐ Most students like Halloween.
Ⓑ Most students like Christmas.
Ⓒ Most students like Thanksgiving.
Ⓓ The students like Easter over Christmas or Thanksgiving.

15. Harper wants to conduct two surveys at his school, where 1,600 students attend. For the first survey, he wants to find out what types of cell phones the students in his school use. Of those students, he wants to survey them to determine their favorite apps. Which of the following is the best method for selecting a random sample?

Ⓐ Select 20 students from each first period class.
Ⓑ Select random students as they enter or exit school.
Ⓒ Select students based on how many text messages they make each month.
Ⓓ Select all of the students.

16. You want to take a survey of 250 people in the mall in one day. You want to create a simple random sample of 100 people. Which method is most likely to result in a simple random sample?

Circle the correct answer choice.

Ⓐ Assign each person a number, then select every prime number.
Ⓑ Select the first 100 people to complete the survey.
Ⓒ Assign each person a number, then select 100 random numbers.
Ⓓ Select 100 people close to the bookstore.

17. Your school is thinking about starting a drama club but they want to know if students like the idea. To sample the population, the principal is going to survey every 10th student that walks into the school on Monday morning starting with the first student.

Circle the method of sampling this describes.

Ⓐ Simple Random Sampling
Ⓑ Systematic Sampling
Ⓒ Convenience Sampling

CHAPTER 4 → Lesson 7: Circle Graphs

1. The circle graph below represents the favorite ice cream flavors of a group of students. If there are 100 students in total, how many students prefer vanilla ice cream? (Use the angle measurements provided in the graph below.)

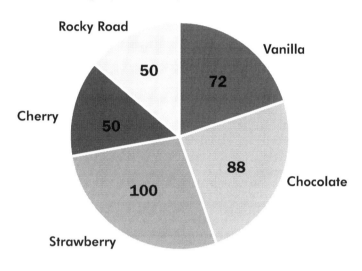

Ⓐ 10
Ⓑ 20
Ⓒ 30
Ⓓ 40

2. A survey was conducted among 210 people to determine their preferred mode of transportation. The circle graph shows the results. Calculate the number of people who prefer biking. (Use the angle measurements provided in the graph below.)

Ⓐ 35
Ⓑ 40
Ⓒ 50
Ⓓ 55

3. The following circle graph shows the distribution of movie genres watched by a group of friends over a month. If the group watched a total of 160 movies, how many movies were of the "Action" genre? (Use the angle measurements provided in the graph below.)

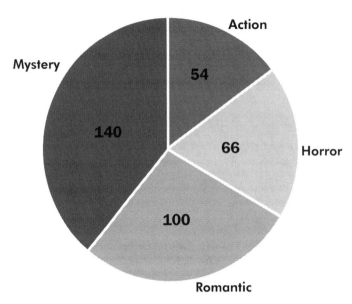

Ⓐ 30
Ⓑ 24
Ⓒ 25
Ⓓ 20

4. A circle graph represents the sales distribution of smartphones in a store. If the total sales amount is $60,000, how much revenue comes from the "Android" category? (Use the angle measurements provided in the graph below.)

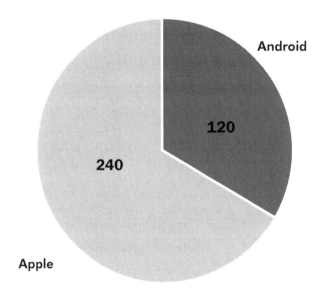

Ⓐ $25,000
Ⓑ $30,000
Ⓒ $40,000
Ⓓ $20,000

5. The circle graph below shows the distribution of time spent on various activities by a student during a day. If the student's total day has 24 hours, how many hours are spent sleeping? Round the number of hours to the nearest whole number. (Use the angle measurements provided in the graph below.)

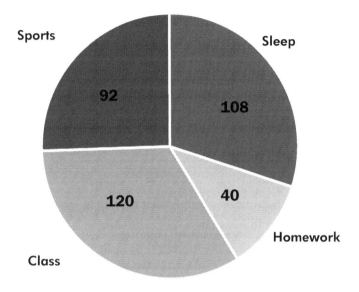

Ⓐ 7 hours
Ⓑ 8 hours
Ⓒ 9 hours
Ⓓ 6 hours

6. In a survey, 250 people were asked about their favorite colors. The circle graph displays the results. How many people chose blue as their favorite color? (Use the angle measurements provided in the graph below.)

Ⓐ 50
Ⓑ 60
Ⓒ 40
Ⓓ 70

7. The circle graph below represents the distribution of students' preferred subjects. If there are 80 students in total, how many students prefer Mathematics? (Use the angle measurements provided in the graph below.)

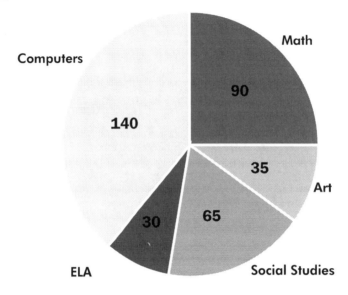

Ⓐ 10
Ⓑ 20
Ⓒ 30
Ⓓ 40

8. A circle graph illustrates the distribution of expenses in a household budget. If the total monthly expenses are $3,000, how much money is spent on transportation? (Use the angle measurements provided in the graph below.)

Ⓐ $600
Ⓑ $700
Ⓒ $800
Ⓓ $900

9. The circle graph represents the distribution of book genres in a library. If there are 600 books in total, how many books belong to the "Science Fiction" genre? Round the number of books to the next integer. (Use the angle measurements provided in the graph below.)

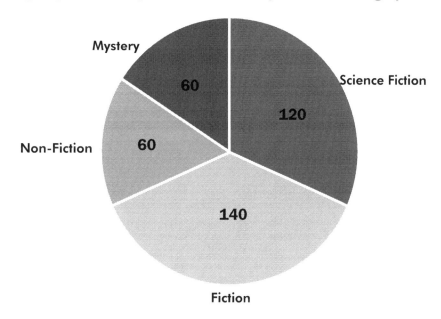

Ⓐ 175
Ⓑ 180
Ⓒ 190
Ⓓ 200

10. A circle graph shows the distribution of dietary preferences among a group of people. If there are 120 participants, how many prefer a vegetarian diet? Round the number of books to the next integer. (Use the angle measurements provided in the graph below.)

Ⓐ 15
Ⓑ 32
Ⓒ 18
Ⓓ 20

CHAPTER 4 → Lesson 8: Graphical Representation of Data

1. You have a data set showing the monthly sales of a retail store over the past year. Which graphical representation is most suitable to show the trend in sales over time?

    Ⓐ Line graph
    Ⓑ Bar Chart
    Ⓒ Histogram
    Ⓓ Dot Plot

2. You want to compare the distribution of ages in a population. Which graphical representation should you use?

    Ⓐ Line graph
    Ⓑ Bar Chart
    Ⓒ Histogram
    Ⓓ Dot Plot

3. You're analyzing survey responses about favorite movie genres. How can you best represent the categorical data?

    Ⓐ Line graph
    Ⓑ Bar Chart
    Ⓒ Histogram
    Ⓓ Dot Plot

4. You're comparing the market share of three competing smartphone brands. Which graphical representation should you use?

    Ⓐ Pie chart
    Ⓑ Bar Chart
    Ⓒ Histogram
    Ⓓ Dot Plot

5. You have data on the number of students who scored within specific score ranges on a test. What type of graph should you use to display this data?

    Ⓐ Pie Chart
    Ⓑ Line Graph
    Ⓒ Histogram
    Ⓓ Vertical bar chart

6. You want to show the relationship between two continuous variables, such as height and weight. What graphical representation is appropriate?

   Ⓐ Scatter plot
   Ⓑ Pie Chart
   Ⓒ Dot Plot
   Ⓓ Histogram

7. You're analyzing the distribution of household incomes in a city. What type of graph is suitable for this data?

   Ⓐ Line Graph
   Ⓑ Pie Chart
   Ⓒ Bar Chart
   Ⓓ Box plot

8. You're comparing the sales performance of different products in a retail store. Which graphical representation would be effective?

   Ⓐ Line Graph
   Ⓑ Grouped bar chart
   Ⓒ Box Plot
   Ⓓ Histogram

9. You want to show the percentage of students who passed a test in each grade level. What type of graph should you use?

   Ⓐ Bar chart
   Ⓑ Histogram
   Ⓒ Box Plot
   Ⓓ Dot Plot

10. You're analyzing the distribution of temperatures recorded each day for a month. Which graphical representation is suitable?

   Ⓐ Histogram
   Ⓑ Dot Plot
   Ⓒ Box plot
   Ⓓ Pie Chart

CHAPTER 4 → Lesson 9: Sample Space of an Event

1. **Which of the following represents the sample space for rolling a fair six-sided die?**

   Ⓐ {1, 2, 3, 4, 5, 6}
   Ⓑ {1, 3, 5}
   Ⓒ {Red, Blue, Green}
   Ⓓ {2, 4, 6}

2. **A coin is flipped three times. What is the size of the sample space?**

   Ⓐ 2
   Ⓑ 3
   Ⓒ 6
   Ⓓ 8

3. **You draw a card from a standard deck of 52 playing cards. What is the sample space?**

   Ⓐ {Red, Blue, Green, Yellow}
   Ⓑ {Hearts, Diamonds, Clubs, Spades}
   Ⓒ {Ace, King, Queen, Jack}
   Ⓓ {1, 2, 3, ..., 52}

4. **A spinner has three equal sections labeled A, B, and C. What is the sample space?**

   Ⓐ {A, B}
   Ⓑ {A, B, C}
   Ⓒ {A, A, A}
   Ⓓ {A, B, B}

5. **You are choosing a snack from a vending machine with options: Chips, Candy, Soda, and Gum. What is the sample space?**

   Ⓐ {Snack, Candy}
   Ⓑ {Chips, Candy, Soda, Gum}
   Ⓒ {Salt, Sweet, Bitter, Sour}
   Ⓓ {A, B, C, D}

6. **Two dice are rolled. What is the sample space?**

   Ⓐ {(1, 1), (1, 2), ..., (6, 6)}
   Ⓑ {1, 2, 3, 4, 5, 6}
   Ⓒ {1, 2, 3}
   Ⓓ {Prime numbers less than 7}

7. **You are rolling a pair of dice, one red and one green. What is the sample space?**

   Ⓐ {(1, 1), (1, 2), ..., (6, 6)}
   Ⓑ {H, T}
   Ⓒ {1,2,3,4,5,6}
   Ⓓ {Even, Odd}

8. **You are choosing a letter from the word "SAMPLE." What is the sample space?**

   Ⓐ {S, A, M, P, L, E}
   Ⓑ {S, A, M}
   Ⓒ {P, L, E}
   Ⓓ {Red, Blue, Green}

9. **A bag contains four red marbles and three blue marbles. Two marbles are drawn without replacement. What is the sample space?**

   Ⓐ {RR, BB, RB}
   Ⓑ {Green, Red, Blue}
   Ⓒ {RRR, BBB}
   Ⓓ {R, B}

10. **You are choosing an ice cream flavor from a menu with options: Vanilla, Chocolate, Strawberry, and Mint. What is the sample space?**

    Ⓐ {Ice Cream, Chocolate}
    Ⓑ {Vanilla, Chocolate, Strawberry, Mint}
    Ⓒ {Sweet, Bitter, Sour}
    Ⓓ {Vanilla, Chocolate, Mint}

CHAPTER 4 → Lesson 10: Understanding Probability

1. **Mary has 3 red marbles and 7 yellow marbles in a bag. If she were to remove 2 red and 1 yellow marbles and set them aside, what is the probability of her pulling a yellow marble as her next marble?**

    (A) $\dfrac{1}{6}$

    (B) $\dfrac{1}{7}$

    (C) $\dfrac{7}{10}$

    (D) $\dfrac{6}{7}$

2. **John has a deck of cards (52 cards). If John removes a number 2 card from the deck, what is the probability that he will pick a number 2 card at random?**

    (A) 3 out of 51
    (B) 4 out of 51
    (C) 26 out of 51
    (D) 30 out of 51

3. **Maggie has a bag of coins (8 nickels, 6 quarters, 12 dimes, 20 pennies). If she picks a coin at random, what is the probability that she will pick a quarter?**

    (A) 2 out of 15
    (B) 3 out of 23
    (C) 3 out of 50
    (D) 5 out of 46

4. **Mark has a box of bills (12 ones, 8 tens, 21 twenties, 30 fifties). If he picks a bill at random, what is the probability that he will pick a ten?**

    (A) 8 out of 71
    (B) 8 out of 100
    (C) 10 out of 71
    (D) 7 out of 71

5. Moe has a bowl of nuts (14 pecans, 8 walnuts, 28 almonds, 33 peanuts). If he picks a nut at random, what is the probability that he will pick a peanut?

   (A) 33 out of 70
   (B) 33 out of 80
   (C) 33 out of 100
   (D) 33 out of 83

6. Xavier has a bowl of nuts (14 pecans, 8 walnuts, 28 almonds, 33 peanuts). If he picks out all the pecans, what is the probability that he will pick a walnut at random?

   (A) 8 out of 83
   (B) 8 out of 69
   (C) 8 out of 100
   (D) 8 out of 70

7. Tim has a box of chocolates with the following flavors: 24 cherry, 26 caramel, 20 fudge, and 16 candy. If he picks out two of each type of chocolate, what is the probability that he will pick a cherry chocolate at random?

   (A) 11 out of 35
   (B) 4 out of 13
   (C) 11 out of 50
   (D) 11 out of 39

8. Clarissa has a box of chocolates with the following flavors: 24 cherry, 26 caramel, 20 fudge, and 16 taffy. If she picks out all the taffy, what is the probability that she will pick a fudge chocolate at random?

   (A) 2 out of 7
   (B) 10 out of 43
   (C) 1 out of 5
   (D) 8 out of 35

9. Karen has a box of chocolates with the following flavors: 24 cherry, 26 caramel, 20 fudge, and 16 taffy. If she removes half of the cherry and fudge chocolates from the box, what is the probability that she will pick a taffy chocolate at random?

   (A) 1 out of 4
   (B) 8 out of 43
   (C) 4 out of 25
   (D) 16 out of 43

10. The table below shows the types of fruits Jessie's mom purchased from the grocery store.

Type of Fruit	Number of Fruits
Apple	6
Orange	4
Pear	2
Peaches	3

If Jessie grabs one of the fruits without looking, what is the probability that he will **NOT** pick a peach?

Ⓐ $\dfrac{2}{5}$

Ⓑ $\dfrac{3}{15}$

Ⓒ $\dfrac{4}{5}$

Ⓓ $\dfrac{2}{3}$

11. The table shows the types of books five friends like. One friend is chosen at random. Identify the outcome of the event. Event: The friend that likes non-fiction.

Circle the outcome of the event shown below.

Favorite Types of Books

Ⓐ Friend - Type
Ⓑ Sarah - Fiction
Ⓒ John - Non-Fiction
Ⓓ Billy - Fantasy
Ⓔ Raj - Mystery
Ⓕ Kavi - Romance

12. When one number cube is rolled, the following six outcomes are possible.

Identify the outcomes for each event.

Fill in the blanks given in the table with the correct outcomes.

Event	Outcome
The number cube comes up odd.	1, 3, 5
The number cube comes up even.	
The number cube comes up greater than 3.	
The number cube comes up less than or equal to 5.	

CHAPTER 4 → Lesson 11: Predicting Using Probability

1. **Which of the following represents the sample space for flipping two coins?**

    Ⓐ {HH, TT}
    Ⓑ {H, T}
    Ⓒ {HH, HT, TH, TT}
    Ⓓ {HH, HT, TT}

2. **Which of the following experiments would best test the statement, "The probability of a coin landing on heads is 1/2."?**

    Ⓐ Toss a coin 1,000 times, and record the results.
    Ⓑ Toss a coin twice to see if it lands on heads one out of those two times.
    Ⓒ Toss a coin until it lands on heads and record the number of tries it took.
    Ⓓ Toss a coin twice, if it doesn't land on heads exactly once, the theoretical probability is false.

3. **Which of the following results is most likely from rolling a six-sided die?**

    Ⓐ Rolling an odd number
    Ⓑ Rolling an even number
    Ⓒ Rolling a number from 1 to 3
    Ⓓ All of the above are equally likely.

4. **Sandy flipped a coin 40 times. Her results are 75% heads and 25% tails. What is the difference between the actual results and the expected results?**

    Ⓐ 20%
    Ⓑ 50%
    Ⓒ 25%
    Ⓓ 10%

5. **Maggie rolled a pair of four sided dice 10 times. The results are 30% side 1, 20% side 2, 20% side 3, 30% side 4. What is the difference between the results and the expected results for all four sides?**

    Ⓐ 25% side 1,
        25% side 2,
        25% side 3,
        25% side 4

    Ⓑ 5% side 1,
        5% side 2,
        5% side 3,
        5% side 4

    Ⓒ 5% side 1,
        25% side 2,
        25% side 3,
        5% side 4

    Ⓓ 4% side 1,
        4% side 2,
        4% side 3,
        4% side 4

6. **Maggie rolls two pairs of four sided dice 10 times. The results were 30% side 1, 20% side 2, 20% side 3, 30% side 4. What were the actual results and expected results?**

    Ⓐ Results: 12 side 1, 8 side 2, 8 side 3, 12 side 4 ...Expected Results: 10 side 1, 10 side 2, 10 side 3, 10 side 4
    Ⓑ Results: 6 side 1, 4 side 2, 4 side 3, 6 side 4 ...Expected Results: 5 side 1, 5 side 2, 5 side 3, 5 side 4
    Ⓒ Results: 6 side 1, 4 side 2, 4 side 3, 6 side 4 ...Expected Results: 10 side 1, 10 side 2, 10 side 3, 10 side 4
    Ⓓ Results: 10 side 1, 10 side 2, 10 side 3, 10 side 4 ...Expected Results: 12 side 1, 8 side 2, 8 side 3, 12 side 4

7. **Juliana was expected to make 80% of her first serves in the tennis match. She made half of 60 first serves in the match. What were the results and expected results?**

    Ⓐ Results: 30 first serves. Expected Results: 48 first serves
    Ⓑ Results: 20 first serves. Expected Results: 48 first serves
    Ⓒ Results: 25 first serves. Expected Results: 48 first serves
    Ⓓ Results: 35 first serves. Expected Results: 48 first serves

8. Which of the following represents the sample space for rolling a pair of four-sided dice?

   Ⓐ (1,1) (1,2) (1,3) (1,4) (2,2) (2,3) (2,4) (3,3) (3,4) (4,4)
   Ⓑ (1,2) (1,3) (1,4) (2,3) (2,4) (3,4)
   Ⓒ (1,2) (1,3) (1,4) (2,3) (2,4)(3,4) (4,4)
   Ⓓ (1,2) (1,3) (1,4) (2,3) (2,4)

9. Lea is playing a carnival game and has a chance to win a large stuffed teddy bear. In order to win, she has to guess the color of the cube she will pick out of a box. The box is shown below.

"Pick the Cube" Carnival Game

Based on the colors and number of blocks, what is Lea's chance of winning the game if she says that she will pick a black cube out of the box?

   Ⓐ 60%
   Ⓑ 10%
   Ⓒ 90%
   Ⓓ 40%

10. Ms. Green is passing out snacks during her tutoring session. She has 7 bags of chips, 13 candy bars, 16 fruit snacks, and 10 lollipops. If one of Ms. Green's students randomly selects a snack, what is the probability that he will select a fruit snack? Round your answer to the nearest tenth of a percent.

   Ⓐ 34.8%
   Ⓑ 65.2%
   Ⓒ 16.0%
   Ⓓ 84.0%

11. Mark the correct probabilities for each event.

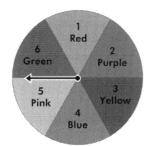

	$\dfrac{1}{6}$	$\dfrac{1}{3}$	$\dfrac{1}{2}$
The probability you spin an odd number.	○	○	○
The probability you spin a 3.	○	○	○
The probability you spin a blue.	○	○	○
The probability you spin a red or yellow.	○	○	○

12. What is the probability that the spinner will stop on the #3 sector?

Circle the correct answer choice.

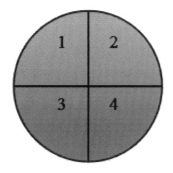

Ⓐ 1.3

Ⓑ $\dfrac{1}{2}$

Ⓒ $\dfrac{1}{3}$

Ⓓ $\dfrac{1}{4}$

CHAPTER 4 → Lesson 12: Using Probability Models

1. **Sara rolls two dice, one black and one yellow. What is the probability that she will roll a 3 on the black die and a 5 on the yellow die?**

   Ⓐ $\dfrac{1}{6}$

   Ⓑ $\dfrac{1}{12}$

   Ⓒ $\dfrac{2}{15}$

   Ⓓ $\dfrac{1}{36}$

2. **Which of the following represents the probability of an event most likely to occur?**

   Ⓐ 0.25
   Ⓑ 0.91
   Ⓒ 0.58
   Ⓓ 0.15

3. **Which of the following is not a valid probability?**

   Ⓐ 0.25

   Ⓑ $\dfrac{1}{5}$

   Ⓒ 1

   Ⓓ $\dfrac{5}{4}$

4. **Tom tosses a coin 12 times. The coin lands on heads only twice. If Tom tosses the coin one more time, what is the probability that the coin will land on heads?**

   Ⓐ 40%
   Ⓑ 50%
   Ⓒ 60%
   Ⓓ 15%

5. Joe has 5 nickels, 5 dimes, 5 quarters, and 5 pennies in his pocket. Six times, he randomly picked a coin from his pocket and put it back. Joe picked a dime every time. If he randomly picks a coin from his pocket again, what is the probability the coin will be a dime?

   Ⓐ 33%
   Ⓑ 100%
   Ⓒ 24%
   Ⓓ 25%

6. Jim rolls a pair of six-sided dice five times. He rolls a pair of two's five times in a row. If he rolls the dice one more time, what is the probability he will roll a pair of fours?

   Ⓐ 1 out of 21
   Ⓑ 1 out of 36
   Ⓒ 1 out of 24
   Ⓓ 1 out of 6

7. Bob rolls a six-sided die and flips a coin five times. He rolls a three and flips the coin to tails five times in a row. If he rolls the die and flips the coin one more time, what is the probability he will roll a three and flip the coin on tails?

   Ⓐ 1 out of 6
   Ⓑ 1 out of 10
   Ⓒ 1 out of 12
   Ⓓ 1 out of 7

8. Mia rolls a pair of six-sided dice and flips two coins ten times. She rolls a pair of threes and flips the coins to tails ten times in a row. If she rolls the dice and flips the coins one more time, what is the probability she will roll all fives and flip the coins on heads?

   Ⓐ 1 out of 60
   Ⓑ 1 out of 144
   Ⓒ 1 out of 128
   Ⓓ 1 out of 64

9. Sophia wants to select a pair of shorts from Too Sweet Clothing Store. The store has 2 different colors of shorts (black (B) and green (G)) available in sizes of small (S), medium (M), and large (L). If Sophia grabs a pair of shorts without looking, which sample space shows the different types of shorts she could select?

   Ⓐ {BS, BM, BL, GS, GM, GL}
   Ⓑ {BB, BG, SS, SM, SL}
   Ⓒ {BG, SM, SL}
   Ⓓ {BS, BL, GS, GL}

10. Eric's Pizza Shop is offering a sale on any large two-topping pizza for $8.00. Customers have a choice between thin crust (T) or pan pizza (Z), one meat topping [pepperoni(P), Italian sausage (I), or ham (H)], and one vegetable topping [green peppers (G), onions (O), or mushrooms (M)]. Which sample space shows the number of possible combinations customers can have if they select a thin crust pizza?

Ⓐ {TPG, TIO, THM}
Ⓑ {TPG, TPO, TPM, TIG, TIO, TIM, THG, THO, THM}
Ⓒ {TPG, TPO, TIG, TIO, THG, THO}
Ⓓ {TPG, TPO, TPM, TIG, TIO, TIM, THG, THO, THM, PPG, PPO, PPM, PIG, PIO, PIM, PHG, PHO, PHM}

11. There is a bag of tiles with 5 black tiles, 5 white tiles, and 5 blue tiles. You are going to choose one tile at random. Are the outcomes of this event equally likely?

Circle the correct answer.

Ⓐ Yes

Ⓑ No

12. You are playing a game using this spinner. You get one spin on each turn. Which list shows a complete probability model for the spinner?

Circle the correct answer.

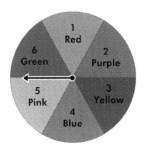

Ⓐ P(even number) = $\dfrac{3}{6}$, P(odd number) = $\dfrac{3}{6}$

Ⓑ P(red) = $\dfrac{1}{6}$, P(blue) = $\dfrac{1}{6}$

Ⓒ P(number <4) = $\dfrac{3}{6}$

Ⓓ P(yellow or green) = $\dfrac{2}{6}$, P(red or blue) = $\dfrac{2}{6}$

CHAPTER 4 → Lesson 13: Probability Models from Observed Frequencies

1. Felix flipped a coin 8 times and got the following results: H, H, T, H, H, T, T, H. If these results were typical for that coin, what are the odds of flipping a heads with that coin?

   Ⓐ 3 out of 5
   Ⓑ 5 out of 8
   Ⓒ 3 out of 8
   Ⓓ 1 out of 2

2. Bridgette rolled a six-sided die 100 times to test the frequency of each number's appearing. According to these statistics, how many times should a 2 be rolled out of 50 rolls?

Number	Frequency
1	18%
2	20%
3	16%
4	11%
5	18%
6	17%

   Ⓐ 10 times
   Ⓑ 20 times
   Ⓒ 12 times
   Ⓓ 15 times

3. Randomly choosing a number out of a hat 50 times resulted in choosing an odd number a total of four more times than the number of times an even number was chosen. How many times was an even number chosen from the hat?

   Ⓐ 27 times
   Ⓑ 21 times
   Ⓒ 29 times
   Ⓓ 23 times

4. 8 out of the last 12 customers at Paul's Pizza ordered pepperoni pizza. According to this data, what is the probability that the next customer will NOT order pepperoni pizza?

   Ⓐ 1 out of 3
   Ⓑ 4 out of 5
   Ⓒ 1 out of 2
   Ⓓ 2 out of 5

5. Susan is selling cookies for a fundraiser. Out of the last 20 people she asked, 10 people bought 1 box of cookies, 5 bought more than 1 box, and 5 bought none. Based on this data, what is the probability that the next person she asks will buy at least 1 box of cookies?

   Ⓐ 1 out of 3
   Ⓑ 2 out of 5
   Ⓒ 4 out of 5
   Ⓓ 3 out of 4

6. William has passed 9 out of his last 10 tests in Spanish class. Based on his past history, what is the probability that he will NOT pass the next test?

   Ⓐ 10%
   Ⓑ 25%
   Ⓒ 15%
   Ⓓ 8%

7. Travis has scored goals in 7 of his last 9 soccer games. At this rate, what is the probability that he will score in his next game? Round the nearest percent.

   Ⓐ 70%
   Ⓑ 17%
   Ⓒ 78%
   Ⓓ 53%

8. Gabe's free throw percentage for the season has been 80%. Based on this, if he has 5 free throws in the next game, how many is he likely to miss?

   Ⓐ 0
   Ⓑ 1
   Ⓒ 2
   Ⓓ 3

9. York and his partner have won the doubles tennis tournament three out of the last four years. According to this record, what is the probability they will win it again this year?

   Ⓐ 3 out of 4
   Ⓑ 1 out of 3
   Ⓒ 1 out of 2
   Ⓓ 4 out of 5

10. Robbie runs track. His finishes for his last 6 events were: 1st, 3rd, 2nd, 5th, 4th, 2nd. Based on these results, what is the probability he will finish in the top 3 of his next event?

Ⓐ 4 out of 5
Ⓑ 2 out of 3
Ⓒ 1 out of 2
Ⓓ 3 out of 4

11. The table shows observed frequencies of spinning a spinner with 4 numbers on it (1, 2, 3, 4).

	Experiment Table				
Outcome	1	2	3	4	50 total trials
Frequency	6	11	19	14	

What is the observed probability of spinning a 4?

Circle the correct answer choice.

Ⓐ $P(4) = \dfrac{2}{7}$

Ⓑ $P(4) = 14$

Ⓒ $P(4) = \dfrac{4}{14}$

Ⓓ $P(4) = \dfrac{7}{25}+$

12. The table shows observed frequencies of rolling a six sided die. Mark the probabilities of different outcomes given in the table.

	Experiment Table						
Outcome	1	2	3	4	5	6	50 total trials
Frequency	7	9	10	8	9	7	

	$\dfrac{24}{50}$	$\dfrac{26}{50}$
Probability of rolling greater than or equal to 4	○	○
Probability of rolling less than 4	○	○
Probability of rolling an even number	○	○
Probability of rolling an odd number	○	○

End of Data Analysis and Probability

Chapter 4
Data Analysis and Probability

Lesson 1: Context of Data Gathered

Question No.	Answer	Detailed Explanations
1	B	Find the total number of newspapers leftover and divide by the number of days. $\frac{3 + 6 + 1 + 0 + 2 + 3 + 6}{7} = \frac{21}{7} = 3$ newspapers
2	D	Find the mean, median, and mode of the data set and compare. Mean: $\frac{13 + 18 + 14 + 12 + 15 + 19 + 11 + 15}{8} = \frac{117}{8} = 14.625$ Median: 11, 12, 13, 14, 15, 15, 18, 19 → 14.5 Mode: 15 Mode > Mean > Median
3	C	Add the temperatures and divide by the number of temperatures. $\frac{67 + 69 + 69 + 70 + 71 + 72 + 73 + 74 + 74 + 75}{10} = \frac{714}{10} = 71.4°F$

Question No.	Answer	Detailed Explanations
4	B	First find the mean.

$$\frac{83 + 92 + 76 + 87 + 89 + 96 + 88 + 91 + 79 + 99}{10} = \frac{880}{10} = 88\%$$

Now find the distance between each number and the average.

$$|83-88|=5$$
$$|92-88|=4$$
$$|76-88|=12$$
$$|87-88|=1$$
$$|89-88|=1$$
$$|96-88|=8$$
$$|88-88|=0$$
$$|91-88|=3$$
$$|79-88|=9$$
$$|99-88|=11$$

Take the average of these differences

$$\frac{5 + 4 + 12 + 1 + 1 + 8 + 0 + 3 + 9 + 11}{10} = \frac{54}{10} = 5.4\%$$

5	A	First find the mean.

$$\frac{12.3 + 12.6 + 12.2 + 10.9 + 11.3 + 10.3 + 11.7 + 10.7}{8} = \frac{92}{8} = 11.5$$

Now find the distance between each number and the average.

$$|12.3-11.5|=0.8$$
$$|12.6-11.5|=1.1$$
$$|12.2-11.5|=0.7$$
$$|10.9-11.5|=0.6$$
$$|11.3-11.5|=0.2$$
$$|10.3-11.5|=1.2$$
$$|11.7-11.5|=0.2$$
$$|10.7-11.5|=0.8$$

Take the average of these differences

$$\frac{0.8 + 1.1 + 0.7 + 0.6 + 0.2 + 1.2 + 0.2 + 0.8}{8} = \frac{5.6}{8} = 0.7min$$

Question No.	Answer	Detailed Explanations
6	A	Put the numbers in order from least to greatest. 72 82 86 93 95 112 122 130 145 Median = 95 $Q1 = \frac{82 + 86}{2} = 84$ $Q3 = \frac{122 + 130}{2} = 126$ IQR = 126 − 84 = 42 M = 95, Q1 = 84, Q3 = 126, IQR = 42
7	D	Put the numbers in order from least to greatest. $0.75 $3.75 $4.15 $5.20 $6.50 Median = $4.15 $Q1 = \frac{0.75 + 3.75}{2} = \$2.25$ $Q3 = \frac{5.20 + 6.50}{2} = \$5.85$ IQR = 5.85 - 2.25 = $3.60 M = $4.15, IQR = $3.60
8	B	Find the average of both and then find the difference. Anna: $\frac{2.60 + 0 + 7.00 + 4.40 + 3.7}{5} = \frac{17.75}{5} = \$3.55$ Monica: $\frac{5.20 + 6.50 + 3.75 + 0.75 + 4.1}{5} = \frac{20.35}{5} = \$4.07$ Difference: $4.07 − $3.55 = $0.52
9	C	Zahra: 3 8 10 11 12 14 $Median = \frac{10 + 11}{2} = \frac{21}{2} = 10.5$ Q1 = 8 Q3 = 12 IQR = 12 − 8 = 4 Tyland: 4 6 7 9 12 18 $Median = \frac{7 + 9}{2} = \frac{16}{2} = 8$ Q1 = 6 Q3 = 12 IQR = 12 − 6 = 6 Tyland has the greater IQR of 6, which is 2 points higher than Zahra's.

Question No.	Answer	Detailed Explanations
10	A	First find the mean. $$\frac{20 + 42 + 15 + 23 + 53 + 62 + 58}{7} = \frac{273}{7} = 39$$ Now find the distance between each number and the average. $$|20-39|=19$$ $$|42-39|=3$$ $$|15-39|=24$$ $$|23-39|=16$$ $$|53-39|=14$$ $$|62-39|=23$$ $$|58-39|=19$$ Take the average of these differences $$\frac{19 + 3 + 24 + 16 + 14 + 23 + 19}{7} = \frac{118}{7} = 16.9 \ customers$$
11	20	To find the median score, order the numbers from least to greatest. 10, 14, 15, 20, 20, 23, 24, 35, 36 Then identify the number that is in the middle. In this list, 20 is in the middle of the list so the median is 20.
12	B	$(13 + 19 + 16 + z + 17) / 5 = 16$ $(65 + z) / 5 = 16$ Multiply both sides by 5, $65 + z = 16 \times 5 = 80$ Subtract 65 from both sides to isolate z $z = 80 - 65 = 15$

Lesson 2: Relating Data Distributions

Question No.	Answer	Detailed Explanations
1	D	False. There is not enough information to determine the mode score.
		False. There are 14 out of 36 students who received an 81% or higher. This is less than a half of the students.
		False. Twelve students received a 70% or lower.
		True. We know that the median score (the average of the 18th and 19th number) falls between 71% and 80% but we do not know the specific value.
2	A	A) True. The store carries 13 basketball and 5 climbing shoe types for a total of 18 types. This is greater than 15 types, the number of running shoe types.
		B) False. The graph does not give any information about how much is sold.
		C) False. The store has 9 types of walking shoes and 10 types of cross trainers and thus has more types of cross trainers than walking shoes.
		D) False. The graph does not give any information about how much is sold.
3	C	A) False. The weights of Milo's fish have less variability as shown by the closeness of his data points.
		B) False. The average weight of Milo's fish is $\frac{1.2 + 1.2 + 1.5 + 1.6 + 1.6 + 1.7 + 1.8 + 1.8}{8} = \frac{12.4}{8} = 1.55$ *pounds*. The average weight of Jacque's fish is $\frac{1+1.2+1.2+1.5+1.7+1.8+2+2}{8} = \frac{12.4}{8} = 1.55$ *pounds*. Hence the average weights are the same.
		C) True. Without any calculations, you can see that Jacque's fish have weights that are farther away from the mean of 1.55 lbs than Milo's fish weight data.
		D) False. Milo and Jacque caught the same weight in fish. See (B) above.

Question No.	Answer	Detailed Explanations
4	B	A) False. $17 + 20 + 9 + 8 + 12 + 4 = 70$ students
		B) True. $\dfrac{[17(11) + 20(12) + 9(13) + 8(14) + 12(15) + 4(16)]}{70} = \dfrac{900}{70} = 12.86$
		C) False. The current median age is the average of the 35th and 36th numbers which is $\dfrac{12 + 12}{2} = 12$. If three sixteen year olds arrived the median number would be the 37th number which is 12. Therefore the median age would not change.
		D) False. There are 33 students older than the mean of 12.86. Half of 70 would be 35 and 33 is less than 35. Therefore less than half of the students are older than the median.
5	B	A) False. The best fuel mileage recorded was 38 mpg.
		B) True. The Interquartile range is from $27 - 34$ mpg which contains 50% of the data.
		C) False. The median fuel mileage was 31 mpg.
		D) False. There are twelve data points in all which means that each quartile contains four points and the IQR contains two quartiles or eight points.
6	D	Note: Each tick mark is 2 inches.
		A) False. About 25% of the trees were 7 feet 6 inches or taller.
		B) False. Each quartile has the same number of data points.
		C) False. The median height is 6 feet 4 inches.
		D) True. If Q3 has 15 data points then so do Q1, Q2 and Q4. This makes a total of $15 * 4 = 60$ trees. We say "about" because the median may not be in a quartile.
7	C	A) False. There are 27 leaves which represent data for 27 students.
		B) False. The median number is the 14th number. This is 54.
		C) True. The greatest number of jumping jacks performed was 72 and the least was 30. $72 - 30 = 42$.
		D) False. There are six leaves in the 3 (30) stem which represents 6 students who performed less than 40 jumping jacks.

Question No.	Answer	Detailed Explanations
8	D	A) False The current mean of Tamryn's data is $\frac{[2(4) + 4(6) + 2(10) + 2(12)]}{10}$ $= \frac{76}{10} = 7.6$. If a 10 were added the new mean would be $\frac{[2(4) + 4(6) + 2(10) + 2(12) + 10]}{11} = \frac{86}{11} = 7.6$.
		B) False. Tamryn: $\frac{[2(4) + 4(6) + 2(10) + 2(12)]}{10} = \frac{76}{10} = 7.8$. Clio: $\frac{[2(6) + 2(7) + 3(8) + 9 + 2(10)]}{10} = \frac{79}{10} = 7.9$. Clio used more beads than Tamryn on the average.
		C) False. As shown by the spread of the data, Tamryn's data has more variability than Clio's.
		D) True. The median of Clio's data is 8. If Clio added another 8 the median would remain the same.
9	A	A) True. There are a total of $2 + 5 + 18 + 4 + 1 = 30$ days. 18 of these days had a temperature of $70 - 74°F$. This is more than half of the days.
		B) False. $4 + 1 = 5$ days had temperatures above $74°F$. This is $\frac{5}{30}$ $= 16.6\%$ which is less than 20%.
		C) False. There is no way to determine the average temperature without specific data points.
		D) False. There were $5 + 2 = 7$ days below $74°F$ and $4 + 1 = 5$ days above $74°F$. Therefore there were more days below $74°F$ than days above $74°F$.
10	B	A) False. The mean is $\frac{4 + 6 + 9 + 10 + 13 + 14 + 17 + 17 + 17 + 18 + 20 + 20 + 22 + 22 + 25 + 31 + 34}{17} = \frac{299}{17}$ $= 17.59$. The median is 17. Therefore the mean is greater than the median.
		B) True. The middle number is 17.
		C) False. The range of fireflies is $34 - 4 = 30$.
		D) False. Marcel caught fireflies on 17 nights.

Question No.	Answer	Detailed Explanations
11	Box 3	Because box 3 shows that 6 students in this class have 3 siblings. A smaller number of students have 0, 1, 2, 4, 5, or 6 siblings in this class.

	10	14	17
Team 1: 15, 16, t, 17, 12, Mode = 17, What is t?			O
Team 2: 7, 14, r, 16, 13 Mean = 12, What is r?	O		
Team 3: 11, 7, 19, 14, z, Median = 14, What is z?		O	

Team 1: t =17 would be the mode because it would be listed two times.

Team 2: $(7 + 14 + r + 16 + 13) / 5 = 12$

$(50 + r) = 12 \times 5 = 60$

$r = 60 - 50 = 10$

Team 3: Arrange the known numbers in ascending order : 7, 11, 14, 19. It is given median is 14. Therefore, the unknown number z must be more than or equal to 14.

$z = 14$

Lesson 3: Mean, Median, and Mean Absolute Deviation

Question No.	Answer	Detailed Explanations
1	C	There is a strong positive correlation between the height and the weight because there is an upward trend in the weight as a person gets taller.
2	C	When analyzing the heights of the basketball players and soccer players, the average height of the basketball players is 5'4, and the average height of the soccer players is 5'2. Therefore, the average height of the basketball players is higher than the average height of the soccer players.
3	D	Remember: the mean represents the average of the values, which is calculated by adding all the values together then dividing by the number of values you added. In this case, $\frac{24 + 36 + 55 + 65}{2} =$ 45, and $\frac{72 + 78}{2} = 75$. The difference between these two values is 30, as indicated.
4	A	Remember: A mean is the average of all the data presented. In this case, you have to average the temperatures, then replace the January temperature with 54 and recalculate the average, then take the difference. Another way of solving the problem is as follows: January temperature has increased by 54 - 24 = 30 degrees. So, this 30 degrees is to be distributed equally among all the six months. Therefore the average temperature increases by $\frac{30}{6} = 5$ degrees.
5	D	Remember: the mode of a set of data is the number that occurs most frequently. For this set of data, that number is 9.
6	C	Remember: Mean is the average, median is the middle-number when data is arranged numerically, and mode is the number that appears most often.
7	B	Mean absolute deviation is a measure of the distance between each data value and the mean, so it measures variability.
8	C	To find the mean, add the values, and divide that value by the amount of numbers in the data set. (1) The sum is $\frac{30}{4}$ (2) $\frac{30}{4} \div \frac{6}{1}$ = (3) $\frac{30}{4} \times \frac{1}{6} = \frac{30}{24}$ (the GCF of 30 and 24 is 6) (4) $\frac{5}{4}$
9	A	Mean is the average of a set of data; therefore, another word for mean is average.

Question No.	Answer	Detailed Explanations
10	A	To find the median, find the middle number in the data set. One way to find the median is to order the numbers from least to greatest and cross out the numbers until the middle is reached. Here, the middle number is $\frac{1}{3}$. Calculation: To compare fractions, we have to rewrite them with common denominator. Here LCM of 3 and 5 is 15. Rewrite all the fractions with 15 as the denominator. $\frac{4}{5} = \frac{4 \times 3}{5 \times 3} = \frac{12}{15}.$ $\frac{1}{3} = \frac{1 \times 5}{3 \times 5} = \frac{5}{15}.$ $\frac{1}{5} = \frac{1 \times 3}{5 \times 3} = \frac{3}{15}.$ $\frac{2}{3} = \frac{2 \times 5}{3 \times 5} = \frac{10}{15}.$ $\frac{3}{15} < \frac{5}{15} < \frac{10}{15} < \frac{12}{15}.$ Therefore, when we arrange the data in ascending order, we get $\frac{1}{5}, \frac{1}{3}, \frac{1}{3}, \frac{2}{3}, \frac{4}{5}.$ Median is 3rd score, which is $\frac{1}{3}.$
11	C	Mode is the value that appears most in a set of data. The list has a mode of 1 since that number appears most (3 times).
12	A	Remember: Mean is the average, median is the middle number when data is arranged numerically, and mode is the number that appears most often. Since mode is the value that appears most in a set of data, the original list has a mode of 14 because it is the number that appears most (2 times). Find the mean by adding the set of values and dividing by the amount of numbers in the set of data: (1) The sum of 6,8,1,5,11,14 and 14 = 59 (2) $\frac{59}{7}$ = 8.4 To find the median, find the middle number in the data set. One way to find the median is to order the numbers from least to greatest and cross out the numbers until the middle is reached. Here, the middle number is 8.
13	A	Find the mean by adding the set of values and dividing by the amount of numbers in the set of data: (1) The sum of 0.3, 1.2, 2.5, 4.3 = 8.3 (2) $\frac{8.3}{4}$ = 2.1 Therefore, the mean is 2.1.
14	C	To find the median, find the middle number in the data set. One way to find the median is to order the numbers from least to greatest and cross out the numbers until the middle is reached. Here, the middle numbers are 1.2 and 2.5. Add the numbers together and divide by 2. (1) 1.2 + 2.5 = 3.7 (2) 3.7 ÷ 2 = 1.85, which rounds to 1.9. Therefore, the median is 1.9

Question No.	Answer	Detailed Explanations
15	C	To find the mean absolute deviation, (1) find the mean, (2) find the difference between each data value and the mean (since we are interested in deviation only, ignore the negative sign), and (3) average the differences. Here, the mean is 3.4. The difference between the data values and mean are 1.4, 1.6, 3.6, 2.4 and 1.4. The average of the differences is 2.08.
16		

	Median	Mean
Data Set : 9, 8, 7, 4, 5	**7**	6.6
Data Set : 5, 8, 5, 9, 1, 2	5	**5**
Data Set : 1, 2, 8, 1, 3, 3	**2.5**	3

To find the mean, add all of the numbers together and divide by the number of items. To find the median, order the numbers from least to greatest and select the middle number. If there are two middle numbers, take the mean of the two numbers by adding them together and dividing by 2.

| 17 | -3 | The deviation of the minimum is the minimum - the mean. Here, minimum = 2, mean = 5 Therefore, the deviation of the minimum = 2 - 5 = -3 |

Lesson 4: Mean, Median, and Mode

Question No.	Answer	Detailed Explanations
1	B	Out of 16 scores, 13 of 16 are 4 or below. Since the majority of the scores are low, a person can infer that, overall, customers had a bad experience.
2	D	To answer this question, look at the results of the different dishes. Spaghetti: 7 Pizza: 13 Calzone: 9 Baked Ziti: 2 Since only 2 people said that baked ziti was their favorite food, it is the menu item the manager should remove from the menu.
3	A	The measures of central tendency are mean, which is the average of a set of data; median, which is the middle of a set of data, and mode, which is the value which appears most in a set of data.
4	A	To find the mean absolute deviation, (1) find the mean, (2) find the difference between each data value and the mean (since we are interested in deviation only, ignore the negative sign in the difference before taking average), and (3) average the differences. Here, the mean is 2.5. The differences between the data value and the mean are 1.5, 0.5, 0.5, and 1.5. The average is 1.
5	A	Since mode is the value that appears most in a set of data, the original list has two modes of 2 and 13 because each value appears the same number of times. Find the mean by adding the set of values and dividing by the amount of numbers in the set of data: (1) $2 + 2 + 3 + 4 + 6 + 8 + 9 + 10 + 13 + 13 + 16 + 17 = 103$ (2) $\frac{103}{12} = 8.6$ To find the median, find the middle number in the data set. One way to find the median is to order the numbers from least to greatest and cross out the numbers until the middle is reached. Here, the middle numbers are 8 and 9. Add the numbers together, and divide by 2. (1) $8 + 9 = 17$ (2) $17 \div 2 = 8.5$
6	D	Since mode is the value that appears most in a set of data, the original list has two modes of 11 and 23 since each value appears the same number of times. Find the mean by adding the set of values and dividing by the amount of numbers in the set of data: (1) $11 + 11 + 12 + 13 + 15 + 17 + 18 + 20 + 23 + 23 + 26 + 27 = 219$ (2) $\frac{216}{12} = 18$. To find the median, find the middle number in the data set. One way to find the median is to order the numbers from least to greatest and cross out the numbers until the middle is reached. Here, the middle numbers are 17 and 18. Add the numbers together and divide by 2. (1) $17 + 18 = 35$ (2) $35 \div 2 = 17.5$

Question No.	Answer	Detailed Explanations
7	D	Since mode is the value that appears most in a set of data, the original list has two modes of 31 and 54 since each value appears the same number of times. Find the mean by adding the set of values and dividing by the amount of numbers in the set of data: (1) The sum of 31, 31, 32, 33, 35, 37, 38, 41, 54, 54, 57, 58 = 501 (2) $\frac{501}{12}$ = 41.8 To find the median, find the middle number in the data set. One way to find the median is to order the numbers from least to greatest and cross out the numbers until the middle is reached. Here, the middle numbers are 37 and 38. Add the numbers together, and divide by 2. (1) 37 + 38 = 75 (2) 75 ÷ 2 = 37.5
8	A	Since mode is the value that appears most in a set of data, the original list has a mode of 64 since the number appears most (3 times). Find the mean by adding the set of values and dividing by the amount of numbers in the set of data: (1) The sum of 41, 41, 42, 43, 45, 47, 48, 51, 64, 64, 67, 64 = 617 (2) $\frac{617}{12}$ = 51.4 To find the median, find the middle number in the data set. One way to find the median is to order the numbers from least to greatest and cross out the numbers until the middle is reached. Here, the middle numbers are 47 and 48. Add the numbers together, and divide by 2. (1) 47 + 48 = 95 (2) 95 ÷ 2 = 47.5
9	B	Since mode is the value that appears most in a set of data, the original list has a mode of 54 since the number appears most (3 times). Find the mean by adding the set of values and dividing by the amount of numbers in the set of data: (1) The sum of 51, 51, 52, 53, 55, 57, 58, 61, 54, 54, 57, 54 = 657 (2) $\frac{657}{12}$ = 54.8 To find the median, find the middle number in the data set. One way to find the median is to order the numbers from least to greatest and cross out the numbers until the middle is reached. Here, the middle numbers are 54 and 54. Add the numbers together, and divide by 2. (1) 54 + 54 = 108 (2) 108 ÷ 2 = 54
10	A	Since mode is the value that appears most in a set of data, the original list has a mode of 61 since the number appears most (3 times). Find the mean by adding the set of values and dividing by the amount of numbers in the set of data: (1) The sum of 61, 61, 52, 53, 65, 67, 58, 61, 64, 64, 57, 54 = 717 (2) $\frac{717}{12}$ = 59.8 To find the median, find the middle number in the data set. One way to find the median is to order the numbers from least to greatest and cross out the numbers until the middle is reached. Here, the middle numbers are 61 and 61. Add the numbers together, and divide by 2. (1) 61 + 61 = 122 (2) 122 ÷ 2 = 61

Question No.	Answer	Detailed Explanations
11	C	Since mode is the value that appears most in a set of data, the original list has two modes -- 71 and 74 -- since those numbers appear most (3 times). Find the mean by adding the set of values and dividing by the amount of numbers in the set of data: (1) The sum of 71, 71, 62, 63, 75, 77, 68, 71, 74, 74, 67, 74 = 847 (2) $\frac{847}{12}$ = 70.6 (when rounded to the nearest tenth). To find the median, find the middle number in the data set. One way to find the median is to order the numbers from least to greatest and cross out the numbers until the middle is reached. Here, the middle numbers are 71 and 71. Add the numbers together and divide by 2. (1) 71 + 71 = 142 (2) 142 ÷ 2 = 71
12	A	Since mode is the value that appears most in a set of data, the original list has two modes -- 71 and 74 -- since those numbers appear most (2 times). Find the mean by adding the set of values and dividing by the amount of numbers in the set of data: (1) The sum of 61, 71, 52, 63, 65, 77, 58, 71, 64, 74, 57, 74 = 787 (2) $\frac{787}{12}$ = 65.6 To find the median, find the middle number in the data set. One way to find the median is to order the numbers from least to greatest and cross out the numbers until the middle is reached. Here, the middle numbers are 64 and 65. Add the numbers together, and divide by 2. (1) 64 + 65 = 129 (2) 129 ÷ 2 = 64.5
13	B	Since mode is the value that appears most in a set of data, the original list has a mode of 44 since that number appears most (3 times). Find the mean by adding the set of values and dividing by the amount of numbers in the set of data: (1) The sum of 21, 21, 22, 23, 35, 37, 38, 41, 44, 44, 47, 44 = 417 (2) $\frac{417}{12}$ = 34.8 To find the median, find the middle number in the data set. One way to find the median is to order the numbers from least to greatest and cross out the numbers until the middle is reached. Here, the middle numbers are 37 and 38. Add the numbers together, and divide by 2. (1) 37 + 38 = 75 (2) 75 ÷ 2 = 37.5

Question No.	Answer	Detailed Explanations
14	C	Selecting 108 is the result of finding the sum of the six values in the table and dividing by 6. Selecting 110 results from choosing the mean per day the company needs to make a profit. A mean of 222 results from a calculation error when adding or subtracting the sum of the values and the needed number of visitors. The mean is the average of the values in a set of data. In order for Kelli's Ice Cream Shop to have a mean of 110 per day, multiply 110 times the number of days. 110 x 7 = 770. Kelli's Ice Cream Shop needs 770 visitors per week to make a profit. Add the number of visitors from the table: 63 + 77+ 121 + 96 + 137 + 154 = 648. Subtract the sum from 770. 770 - 648 = 122 Therefore, Kelli's needs 122 visitors on Saturday in order to have a mean of 110 visitors per day for the week and to turn a profit.
15	C	Since mode is the value that appears most in a set of data, the original list has no mode since each value appears the same number of times. If 90 is added to the list, the score would appear twice. Therefore, the mode would be 90. We cannot say anything about mode i.e. whether mode has increased or decreased. So, option (A) is incorrect. The mean would neither increase nor decrease. The mean of the original list is 90, so adding a value of 90 would not change the mean. In the original list, the middle value of the numbers is 89. By adding 90 to the list, there will be two middle values, 89 and 90. The sum of the two middle values is 179. Divide the sum by 2. The quotient, 89.5, is the new median. Therefore, the median will increase by adding 90 to the list.
16		(see table and explanation below)

	Mean	Median	Mode
6	●		
5.5		●	
5			●

To find the mean, add all of the numbers together and divide by the number of items. To find the median, order the numbers from least to greatest and select the middle number. If there are two middle numbers, take the mean of the two numbers by adding them together and dividing by 2. Mode is the number that occurs most often.

$$\text{Mean} = \frac{4 + 5 + 5 + 6 + 7 + 9}{6} = \frac{36}{6} = 6$$

$$\text{Median} = \frac{(3\text{rd score} + 4\text{th score})}{2} = \frac{(5+6)}{2} = \frac{11}{2} = 5.5$$

Mode = 5 (the score 5 has appeared twice)

Question No.	Answer	Detailed Explanations
17	40	Interquartile range (IQR) is the difference between the third and the first quartiles in descriptive statistics. So, you order the numbers from least to greatest: 16.6 22.4 32.6 49.3 51.8 68.2 72.6 98.5 99.8. There are 9 scores. 51.8 is the 5th score, which is the median. To find the first quartile and third quartile, include 51.8 in both the first half and the second half.
		First half : 16.6, 22.4, 32.6, 49.3, 51.8. First quartile is the middle score of the first half, which is, 32.6.
		Second half : 51.8, 68.2, 72.6, 98.5, 99.8. Third quartile is the middle score of the second half , which is, 72.6.
		Therefore, Interquartile range (QR) = 72.6 - 32.6 = 40.

Lesson 5: Sampling a Population

Question No.	Answer	Detailed Explanations
1	C	A group of randomly selected students in the hallways would produce the least amount of bias because it is unlikely for assumptions to be made or factors that influence the data to be present. For example, students in the 8th grade may be taller than other students in other grades, skewing the data toward a higher average. A similar assumption can be made about students on the basketball team. Joe and Mary would already have an idea of the height of their friends.
2	A	A random, representative group represents the people to survey in a population because each person in the population has an equal chance of being included and there is less of a chance of bias altering the results of the survey.
3	C	As the size of the sample (people surveyed) increases, the results become more accurate. Therefore, increasing the sample size increases the reliability of the results.
4	D	Surveying everyone would produce reliable results because there would be specific data from each person; however, due to the length of time needed, among other reasons, surveying everyone may not be possible (depending on the reasons for the survey).
5	B	A sample size gets information from a small group from the population. Since the sample size is supposed to represent the population at large, it's important to know the parameters of the sample size in order to determine how reliable the results are for a given survey.
6	B	An assumption can be made that students on the basketball team are likely to be taller than other students at the school, which can influence the results (make it appear that the average height of the general school population is higher than it actually is). Therefore, calculating the average height of the basketball team would most likely produce the most amount of bias.
7	B	Multiple choice questions are useful for statistical results because they can represents different amounts of data that can be separated into categories and sub-categories based on the type of survey and the intended outcome.
8	C	Bias in collecting data can be caused by using questions where there are likely to be assumptions made or factors that influence the data. A survey that asks questions that cause individuals to answer in a certain way makes assumptions and influences the outcome of the data. Therefore, using that type of survey does not avoid bias.

Question No.	Answer	Detailed Explanations
9	B	When analyzing the data, out of the 10 responses, none of the responses have been less than 6. Therefore, a surprising response from the next person would be a 5 since it is outside the range.
10	B	When analyzing the data, out of the 10 responses, all are within the range of 6 to 8. Therefore, a surprising response from the next person would be a 10 since it is outside of the range.
11	A	Bias in collecting data can be caused by using questions where there are likely to be assumptions made or factors that influence the data. An anonymous survey would encourage individuals to answer questions openly without worry about the implications of their answers. Therefore, an anonymous survey is the best way to avoid receiving biased data.
12	A	Multiple choice questions are useful for statistical results because they can represent different amounts of data that can be separated into categories and sub-categories based on the type of survey and the intended outcome. The optional comments section gives an individual the opportunity to make open observations (without bias). A survey with too many free response questions would be hard to analyze and personal questions invite bias.
13	A	For collecting personal data, an anonymous survey would encourage individuals to answer questions openly without worry about the implications of their answers. It is also a way to avoid receiving bias data. Therefore, a receipt should have a link to an online survey where individuals can enter information about personal data.
14	A	In order to get a reliable, random sample based on the population (players who use the game), the surveyors should set up their survey at the end of a level or section of the game. Players are more likely to answer the survey before going to the next level. People are ready to play at the beginning of a game and ready to turn the game off near the end, so there is a good chance they won't complete the survey. A separate survey is likely to be ignored.
15	C	When choosing a sample to survey for data, the sample should be representative of the target population. Here, the target population is people most likely to purchase music online. These people are most likely to communicate with others about music online. Therefore, an online survey on music social networking websites would give them the best sample.

Question No.	Answer	Detailed Explanations
16		

	Convenience Sample	Systematic Sample	Simple Random Sample
A person chooses every 5th person on a list of names starting with #1.	○	●	○
A person accepts the first 15 people to respond to a magazine ad.	●	○	○
A person picks names out of a hat.	○	○	●

Systematic sampling is a type of probability sampling method in which sample members from a larger population are selected according to a random starting point and a fixed, periodic interval.

Convenience sampling is a statistical method of drawing representative data by selecting people because of the ease of their volunteering or selecting units because of their availability or easy access.

A simple random sample is a subset of a statistical population in which each member of the subset has an equal probability of being chosen. A simple random sample is meant to be an unbiased representation of a group.

Question No.	Answer	Detailed Explanations
17	30	If the representative sample is 10 then you would multiply the number of gray marbles by 5 to get the approximate number of gray marbles. 6 x 5 = 30.

Lesson 6: Describing Multiple Samples

Question No.	Answer	Detailed Explanations
1	B	A group of randomly selected strangers in different places of a mall would produce the least amount of bias because there is unlikely to be assumptions made or factors that influence the data.
2	A	In the survey, 83 students selected science as their favorite subject while the other subjects had a combined number of 94 students. Therefore, an inference can be made that students prefer science over the other subjects.
3	A	In the sample, a combined 93 students chose action movies, 41 students chose drama, and 73 chose comedy. Therefore, an inference can be made that students prefer action movies to other types of movies.
4	A	In the sample, a combined 84 students chose strawberries, 38 students chose bananas and 63 chose blueberries. Therefore, an inference can be made that students prefer strawberries to other types of fruit.
5	A	In the sample, a combined 295 students chose basketball, 106 students chose soccer, and 46 students chose play tennis. Since more students chose basketball, an inference can be made that most students like basketball over soccer or tennis.
6	A	In the sample, a combined 198 students chose summer, 257 students chose fall, and 494 students chose spring. Since more students chose spring, an inference can be that most students prefer the Spring season over Summer or Fall.
7	D	In the sample, a combined 295 students chose pineapple, 238 students chose extra cheese, and 467 students chose pepperoni. Since more students chose pepperoni, an inference can be that most students prefer pepperoni over pineapple or extra cheese.
8	B	In the sample, a combined 95 students chose Game X, 11 students chose Game Y, and 8 students chose Game Z. Since more students chose Game X, an inference can be that most students like Game X over Game Y or Game Z.
9	C	In the sample, a combined 243 co-workers play golf, 163 co-workers chose video games, and 256 co-workers chose fishing. Since golf and fishing are outdoor activities, an inference can be made that most of Tom and Bob's co-workers spend a lot of time outside.

Question No.	Answer	Detailed Explanations
10	D	In the sample, a combined 178 students chose Go fish, 24 students chose hearts, and 25 students chose spades. Since more students chose Go fish, an inference can be that most students like Go fish over hearts or spades.
11	C	In the sample, a combined 24 students chose strawberry, 178 students chose rootbeer, and 25 students chose orange. Since more students chose rootbeer, an inference can be made that most students prefer rootbeer over strawberry or orange.
12	C	In the sample, a combined 225 students chose math, 225 students chose English and 225 students chose science. Since the students' answers reflect the same numbers for each subject, an inference can be made that the same number of students like the three subjects equally.
13	B	In the sample, a combined 120 students chose chocolate, 7 students chose strawberry and 27 students chose cookies-n-cream. Since more students chose chocolate, an inference can be made that most students like chocolate over strawberry or cookies-n-cream.
14	D	In the sample, a combined 198 students chose Christmas, 257 students chose Thanksgiving and 494 students chose Easter. Since more students chose Easter, an inference can be made that most students like Easter over Christmas or Thanksgiving.
15	B	A random, representative group represents the people to survey in a population because each person in the population has an equal chance of being included and there is less of a chance of bias altering the results of the survey. Therefore, Harper should select students as they enter and exit the school.
16	C	C is a simple random sample because A is systematic, B is convenience, and D is biased.
17	B	Systematic sampling is a type of probability sampling method in which sample members from a larger population are selected according to a random starting point and a fixed periodic interval.

Hence, the sampling method shown above is Systematic sampling. |

Lesson 7: Circle Graphs

Question No.	Answer	Detailed Explanations
1	B	To find the number of students who prefer vanilla ice cream, we need to determine the fraction of the circle graph that represents vanilla. The angle for vanilla is 72° out of 360° ($\frac{1}{5}$ of the total). Therefore, the number of students who prefer vanilla ice cream is $\frac{1}{5} \times 100 = 20$.
2	A	The angle for biking is 60° out of 360° ($\frac{1}{6}$ of the total). Therefore, the number of people who prefer biking is $\frac{1}{6} \times 210 = 35$.
3	B	The angle for the "Action" genre is 54° out of 360° ($\frac{3}{20}$ of the total). Therefore, the number of "Action" genre movies watched is $\frac{3}{20} \times 160 = 24$.
4	D	The angle for the "Android" category is 120° out of 360° ($\frac{1}{3}$ of the total). Therefore, the revenue from the "Android" category is $\frac{1}{3} \times \$60,000 = \$20,000$.
5	A	The angle for sleeping is 108° out of 360° ($\frac{3}{10}$ of the total). Therefore, the number of hours spent sleeping is $\frac{3}{10} \times 24 = 7.2$ (approximately 7 hours).
6	A	The angle for blue is 72° out of 360° ($\frac{1}{5}$ of the total). Therefore, the number of people who chose blue as their favorite color is $\frac{1}{5} \times 250 = 50$.
7	B	The angle for Mathematics is 90° out of 360° ($\frac{1}{4}$ of the total). Therefore, the number of students who prefer Mathematics is $\frac{1}{4} \times 80 = 20$.

Question No.	Answer	Detailed Explanations
8	A	The angle for transportation is 72° out of 360° ($\frac{1}{5}$ of the total). Therefore, the amount of money spent on transportation is $\frac{1}{5} \times \$3{,}000 = \$600$.
9	D	The angle for "Science Fiction" is 120° out of 360° ($\frac{1}{3}$ of the total). Therefore, the number of books belonging to the "Science Fiction" genre is $\frac{1}{3} \times 600 = 200$.
10	C	The angle for the vegetarian diet is 54° out of 360° ($\frac{3}{20}$ of the total). Therefore, the number of people preferring a vegetarian diet is $\frac{3}{20} \times 120 = 18$.

Lesson 8: Graphical Representation of Data

Question No.	Answer	Detailed Explanations
1	A	A line graph effectively shows the trend in sales over time, making it easy to identify any patterns or fluctuations.
2	C	A histogram displays the distribution of numerical data, such as ages, by dividing the data into intervals (bins) and showing the frequency of data points within each interval.
3	B	A bar chart is suitable for displaying categorical data (movie genres) and their corresponding frequencies or percentages.
4	A	A pie chart effectively illustrates the proportions of different parts (market shares) in relation to a whole (total market).
5	D	A vertical bar chart can display the frequency of students in different score ranges.
6	A	A scatter plot helps visualize the correlation or relationship between two continuous variables.
7	D	A box plot is ideal for displaying the distribution of numerical data, including measures of central tendency and variability.
8	B	A grouped bar chart can compare the sales performance of different products within each category.
9	A	A stacked bar chart visually displays the composition of a whole (total students) broken down by different components (passed and failed) within each category (grade level).
10	C	A box plot effectively displays the distribution of temperatures, showing median, quartiles, and potential outliers.

Lesson 9: Sample Space of an Event

Question No.	Answer	Detailed Explanations
1	A	The sample space for rolling a fair six-sided die includes the numbers 1 through 6.
2	D	Since each coin flip has 2 possible outcomes (H or T), the total number of outcomes for three flips is $2^3 = 8$.
3	B	The sample space for drawing a card from a standard deck consists of the four suits: Hearts, Diamonds, Clubs, and Spades.
4	B	The sample space for spinning the spinner consists of the three possible outcomes: A, B, and C.
5	B	The sample space for choosing a snack includes the four possible options: Chips, Candy, Soda, and Gum.
6	A	The sample space for rolling two dice consists of all possible pairs of outcomes from the two rolls.
7	A	The sample space for rolling a pair of dice consists of all possible combinations of outcomes from the two dice.
8	A	The sample space for choosing a letter from "SAMPLE" includes the six possible letters.
9	A	The sample space for drawing two marbles without replacement includes all possible orders of drawing red and blue marbles.
10	B	The sample space for choosing an ice cream flavor includes the four possible options.

Lesson 10: Understanding Probability

Question No.	Answer	Detailed Explanations
1	D	Mary originally had 10 marbles in her bag. When she removed 3 marbles, she had 7 remaining marbles. Six of those marbles are yellow. Probability is: (chance of successful outcome)/(total number of outcomes). Plug in the numbers, and solve. 6 chances to pick yellow out of 7 outcomes $= \dfrac{6}{7}$
2	A	There are four number 2 cards in a deck of 52. If one number 2 card is removed, that leaves three number 2 cards out of 51 cards. Probability is: (chance of successful outcome)/(total number of outcomes). Therefore, there is a 3 out of 51 chance that John will pick number 2 at random.
3	B	Maggie has a total of 46 coins, 6 of which are quarters. Probability is: $\dfrac{\text{chance of successful outcome}}{\text{total number of outcomes}}$. Therefore, there is a 6 out of 46 chance that Maggie will pick a quarter. This simplifies to 3 out of 23.
4	A	Mark has a total of 71 bills, 8 of which are tens. Probability is: $\dfrac{\text{chance of successful outcome}}{\text{total number of outcomes}}$. Therefore, there is an 8 out of 71 chance that Mark will pick a ten.
5	D	Moe has a total of 83 nuts, 33 of which are peanuts. Probability is: $\dfrac{\text{chance of successful outcome}}{\text{total number of outcomes}}$. Therefore, there is a 33 out of 83 chance that Moe will pick a peanut.
6	B	Xavier has a total of 83 nuts, 8 of which are walnuts. If he removes the pecans, he will have 69 nuts remaining (83 - 14 = 69). Probability is: $\dfrac{\text{chance of successful outcome}}{\text{total number of outcomes}}$. Therefore, there is an 8 out of 69 chance that Xavier will pick a walnut.
7	D	Tim had a total of 86 chocolates. If he removes 2 of each type of chocolate, he will have 22 cherry, 24 caramel, 18 fudge, and 14 candy remaining for a total of 78 chocolates. Probability is: $\dfrac{\text{chance of successful outcome}}{\text{total number of outcomes}}$ Therefore, there is a 22 out of 78 chance that Tim will pick a cherry chocolate. This reduces to 11 out of 39.

Question No.	Answer	Detailed Explanations
8	A	Clarissa had a total of 86 chocolates. If she removes all of the taffy, she will have 70 chocolates remaining. Probability is: $\frac{\text{chance of successful outcome}}{\text{total number of outcomes}}$ Therefore, there is a 20 out of 70 chance that Clarissa will pick a fudge chocolate. This reduces to 2 out of 7.
9	A	Karen had a total of 86 chocolates. If she removes $\frac{1}{2}$ of the cherry and fudge chocolates, she will have 12 cherry, 26 caramel, 10 fudge, and 16 taffy remaining for a total of 64 chocolates. Probability is: $\frac{\text{chance of successful outcome}}{\text{total number of outcomes}}$. Therefore, there is a 16 out of 64 chance that Karen will pick a taffy chocolate. This reduces to 1 out of 4.
10	C	Probability of Jessie picking up a peach is $\frac{3}{15}$, subtract that amount from $\frac{15}{15}$ (Probability of picking one fruit of any type = 1 = $\frac{15}{15}$). $\frac{15}{15}$ - $\frac{3}{15}$ = $\frac{12}{15}$, which in simplest form is $\frac{4}{5}$. Therefore, the probability that he will not pick a peach is $\frac{4}{5}$.
11	C	An event is a group of one or more possible outcomes. The outcome John satisfies the event of choosing Non-Fiction.

12			

Event	Outcome
The number cube comes up odd.	1, 3, 5
The number cube comes up even.	2,4,6
The number cube comes up greater than 3.	4,5,6
The number cube comes up less than or equal to 5.	1,2,3,4,5

The answers are :
1) The number cube comes up even - 2,4,6
2) The number cube comes up greater than 3 - 4,5,6
3) The number cube comes up less than or equal to 5 - 1,2,3,4,5
This answer requires the identification of odd, even, greater than 3 & less than or equal to 5 outcomes.

Lesson 11: Predicting Using Probability

Question No.	Answer	Detailed Explanations
1	C	Create a sample space by listing all the possible outcomes. For each coin flipped, it will land on heads or tails. Therefore, for two coins, there could be outcomes of (heads, heads), (heads, tails), (tails, heads), and (tails, tails).
2	A	When testing probability, larger samples (experiments) yield more accurate results. An experiment of 1,000 coin tosses could adequately test if a coin would land on its head $\frac{1}{2}$ of the time (about 500 of 1,000).
3	D	Since there are three even numbers (2, 4, 6) and three odd numbers (1, 3, 5) on a six-sided die, the probability is 3 out of 6 for rolling either an even or an odd number. Therefore, it is equally likely to roll an even or odd number. There is also a 3 out of 6 chance of rolling a number from 1 to 3.
4	C	The theoretical probability (expected outcome) of flipping a coin is 1 out of 2 because it will either land on heads or tails (those are the two possible outcomes). 1 out of 2 is equivalent to 50%. Subtract the expected outcome from the actual outcome 75% (75 - 50 = 25) and add the percent sign: 25%
5	B	The theoretical probability (expected outcome) of rolling each die is 1 out of 4 because it will either land on 1, 2, 3 or 4 (those are the four possible outcomes). One out of 4 is equal to 25%. Therefore, the difference between the expected results and the actual results is 5% for each side.
6	A	The theoretical probability (expected outcome) of rolling each die is 1 out of 4 because it will either land on 1, 2, 3 or 4 (those are the four possible outcomes). So, the expected outcome would be 10 for each side. The actual outcome was 40(0.30) for side one and side four and 40(.20) for side two and side three, which equals 12 side one, 8 side two, 8 side three, and 12 side four.
7	A	If Juliana made 60 serves, multiply 60 by the decimal form of 80% to find her expected first serve number. 60 × .80 = 48 first serves expected. If she only made half of the serves, divide 60 by 2. 60 ÷ 2 = 30 actual serves made.
8	A	Create a sample space by listing all the possible outcomes. Combining duplicate outcomes leaves 10 possible results: (1,1) (1,2) (1,3) (1,4) (2,2) (2,3) (2,4) (3,3) (3,4) (4,4)

Question No.	Answer	Detailed Explanations
9	D	There are 10 black cubes in the box and 25 total cubes. Therefore, Lea has a 10 out of 25 chance to pick a black cube. Multiply both 10 and 25 by 4 in order to find out her chances in percent form. 10 x 4 = 40 and 25 x 4 = 100. Since there is a 40 out of 100 chance to pick a black cube, Lea's chances of winning the game is 40%.
10	A	Since there are 16 fruit snacks out of a total of 46 total snacks, the probability of randomly picking a fruit snack is 16 out of 46. Divide 16 by 46, and then multiply by 100 in order to find the probability in percent form. 16 ÷ 46 = 0.3478 x 100 = 34.78%. Rounding to the nearest tenth means a probability of 34.8% that a student will randomly select a fruit snack.

11

	$\frac{1}{6}$	$\frac{1}{3}$	$\frac{1}{2}$
The probability you spin an odd number.			●
The probability you spin a 3.	●		
The probability you spin a blue.	●		
The probability you spin a red or yellow.		●	

(1) Total number of possible outcomes = 6. Number of favorable outcomes (you spin a odd number) = 3 (it may be 1, or 3 or 5).
Therefore Probability = (number of favorable outcomes) / (total number of possible outcomes) = 3/6 = 1/2

(2) Total number of possible outcomes = 6. Number of favorable outcomes (you spin the number 3) = 1
Therefore Probability = (number of favorable outcomes) / (total number of possible outcomes) = 1/6

(3) Total number of possible outcomes = 6. Number of favorable outcomes (you spin a blue) = 1
Therefore Probability = (number of favorable outcomes) / (total number of possible outcomes) = 1/6

(4) Total number of possible outcomes = 6. Number of favorable outcomes (you spin a red or yellow) = 2
Therefore Probability = (number of favorable outcomes) / (total number of possible outcomes) = 2/6 = 1/3

| 12 | D | The probability is the number of favorable outcomes over the number of outcomes in a sample space.
Here, number of favorable outcomes = 1, number of outcomes in the sample space = 4
Therefore probability = $\frac{1}{4}$ |

Lesson 12: Using Probability Models

Question No.	Answer	Detailed Explanations
1	D	Remember: In a compound and event, you can multiply the probabilities of each event in order to arrive at a final solution. There is a $\frac{1}{6}$ chance she will roll a 3 and a $\frac{1}{6}$ chance Sara rolls a 5. This means there is a $\frac{1}{6}(\frac{1}{6}) = \frac{1}{36}$ chance she will roll both. Another way to approach this problem is to create the sample space containing all possible combinations. (B, Y): (1,1), (1,2), (1,3), (1,4), (1,5), (1,6) (2,1), (2,2), (2,3), (2,4), (2,5), (2,6) (3,1), (3,2), (3,3), (3,4), (3,5), (3,6) (4,1), (4,2), (4,3), (4,4), (4,5), (4,6) (5,1), (5,2), (5,3), (5,4), (5,5), (5,6) (6,1), (6,2), (6,3), (6,4), (6,5), (6,6) From this list it is clear that only one out of the 36 total possible matches the (3,5) described.
2	B	Probability is defined as chance that an event will occur (a number between 0 and 1). The closer a probability is to 1, the more likely it is to occur. Drawing a number line with marks 0.1 distance apart can help determine the likelihood of an event occurring. Since 0.91 is close to 1, it represents an event most likely to occur.
3	D	Probability is defined as the chance that an event will occur (a number from 0 to 1). Since $\frac{5}{4}$ is a rational number greater than 1, it cannot represent a probability.
4	B	Theoretical probability is the (number of possible favorable outcomes)/(total number of outcomes). Each time Tom flips a coin, there is 1 possible favorable outcome (heads) out of 2 total possible outcomes. Therefore, the probability is $\frac{1}{2}$, which is equivalent to 50%.
5	D	Since there are the same amount of coins in each amount, the theoretical probability (expected outcome) of picking a coin is 1 out of 4 because Joe will either pick a penny, a nickel, a dime or a quarter. 1 out of 4 is equivalent to 25%.
6	B	For every roll of two 6-sided dice, there are 36 possible outcomes. Therefore, the probability of rolling a pair of fours is 1 out of 36.

Question No.	Answer	Detailed Explanations
7	C	For every roll of a 6-sided die and coin flip, there are 12 possible outcomes: {(1,h), (1,t), (2,h), (2,t), (3,h), (3,t), (4,h), (4,t), (5,h), (5,t), (6,h), (6,t)}. Therefore, the possibility of rolling a three and flipping tails is 1 out of 12.
8	B	For every roll of two 6-sided dice and two coin flips, there are 144 possible outcomes (36 x 4). Therefore, the probability of rolling two fives and flipping two heads is 1 out of 144.
9	A	The sample space of {BS, BM, BL, GS, GM, GL} is the correct answer. Since Sophia has a choice of 2 different pairs of shorts in 3 different combinations, the sample space should reflect choices of black or green shorts in sizes of small, medium, or large.
10	B	For each type of crust, there are 9 possible combinations. Therefore, the sample space {TPG, TPO, TPM, TIG, TIO, TIM, THG, THO, THM} represents the number of combinations if a customer chooses a thin crust pizza.
11	Yes	The outcomes are equally likely because the probability of choosing each color is $\frac{5}{15}$.
12	A	A probability model must add up to equal 1 to account for all possibilities.

Lesson 13: Probability Models from Observed Frequencies

Question No.	Answer	Detailed Explanations
1	B	Because 5 of the 8 times it was flipped, the result was heads, the probability of heads is 5 out of 8.
2	A	If 20% of the rolls result in a 2, then 20% of 50 rolls would be (0.20)(50) = 10 times.
3	D	An even distribution of the odds and evens would be 25 each. 4 more odds would mean 27 odds and 23 evens.
4	A	4 out of 12 customers did NOT order pepperoni. This simplifies to 1 out of 3.
5	D	15 out of the 20 people ordered 1 box or more. This reduces down to 3 out of every 4 people.
6	A	Only 1 time out of 10 did he NOT pass the test, so this is a 10% probability.
7	C	7 out of 9 is a 77.777…% probability, which rounds to 78%.
8	B	An 80% success rate means that he makes 4 out of 5 and misses only 1 out of every 5 free throws.
9	A	The fact that 3 of the last 4 years they won the tournament suggests that this year's probability of winning is that same 3 out of 4.
10	B	4 out of the last 6 results were in the top three, so this simplifies to a 2 out of 3 probability.
11	D	The probability of spinning a 4 is $\frac{14}{50}$, which simplified is $\frac{7}{25}$

Question No.	Answer	Detailed Explanations

12

	$\dfrac{24}{50}$	$\dfrac{26}{50}$
Probability of rolling greater than or equal to 4	●	
Probability of rolling less than 4		●
Probability of rolling an even number	●	
Probability of rolling an odd number		●

Add the frequencies together for each part of the outcome and divide that by the total number of trials.

(1) The probability of rolling greater than or equal to 4 means rolling a 4, 5, or 6. Therefore, the frequencies are 8 + 9 + 7 = 24 out of 50.
(2) The probability of rolling less than 4 means rolling a 1, 2, or 3. Therefore, the frequencies are 7 + 9 + 10 = 26 our of 50.
(3) The probability of rolling an even number means rolling a 2, 4 or 6. Therefore, the frequencies are 9 + 8 + 7 = 24 out of 50.
(4) The probability of rolling an odd number means rolling a 1, 3 or 5. Therefore, the frequencies are 7 + 10 + 9 = 26 out of 50.

Notes

Test Taking Tips

1) **The day before the test,** make sure you get a good night's sleep.
2) **On the day of the test,** be sure to eat a good hearty breakfast! Also, be sure to arrive at school on time.
3) **During the test:**

- **Read every question carefully.**
  - Do not spend too much time on any one question. Work steadily through all questions in the section.
  - Attempt all of the questions even if you are not sure of some answers.
  - If you run into a difficult question, eliminate as many choices as you can and then pick the best one from the remaining choices. Intelligent guessing will help you increase your score.
  - Also, mark the question so that if you have extra time, you can return to it after you reach the end of the section.
  - Some questions may refer to a graph, chart, or other kind of picture. Carefully review the graphic before answering the question.
  - Be sure to include explanations for your written responses and show all work.

- **While Answering EBSR questions.**
  - EBSR questions come in 2 parts - PART A and B.
  - Both PART A and B could be multiple choice or Part A could be multiple choice while Part B could be some other type.
  - Generally, Part A and B will be related, sometimes it may just be from the same lesson but not related questions.
  - If it is a Multiple choice question, Select the bubble corresponding to your answer choice.
  - Read all of the answer choices, even if think you have found the correct answer.
  - In case the questions in EBSR are not multiple choice questions, follow the instruction for other question types while answering such questions.

- **While Answering TECR questions.**
  - Read the directions of each question. Some might ask you to drag something, others to select, and still others to highlight. Follow all instructions of the question (or questions if it is in multiple parts)

Frequently Asked Questions(FAQs)

For more information on 2023-24 Assessment Year, visit
www.lumoslearning.com/a/fast-faqs
OR Scan the **QR Code**

What if I buy more than one Lumos tedBook?

Step 1 → **Visit the link given below and login to your parent/teacher account**

www.lumoslearning.com

Step 2 → <u>For Parent</u>

Click on the horizontal lines (≡) in the top right-hand corner and select **"My tedBooks".** Place the Book Access Code and submit.

<u>For Teacher</u>

Click on "My Subscription" under the "My Account" menu in the left-hand side and select **"My tedBooks".** Place the Book Access Code and submit.

Note: See the first page for access code.

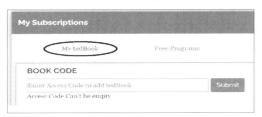

Step 3 → **Add the new book**

To add the new book for a registered student, choose the '**Student**' button and click on submit.

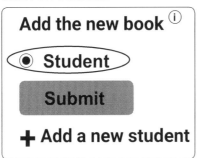

To add the new book for a new student, choose the '**Add New Student**' button and complete the student registration.

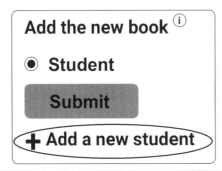

Progress Chart

Standard	Lesson	Score	Date of Completion
BEST			
MA.7.NSO.1.1	Applying Laws of Exponents		
MA.7.NSO.1.2	Solving Multi-Step Problems		
MA.7.NSO.2.1	Rational Numbers, Addition & Subtraction		
MA.7.NSO.2.1	Rational Numbers, Multiplication and Division		
MA.7.NSO.2.2	Strategies for Adding and Subtracting Rational Numbers		
MA.7.NSO.2.2	Strategies for Multiplying and Dividing Rational Numbers		
MA.7.NSO.2.3	Solving Real World Problems		
MA.7.AR.1.1	Applying Properties to Rational Expressions		
MA.7.AR.1.2	Interpreting the Meanings of Expressions		
MA.7.AR.2.1	Linear Inequality Word Problems		
MA.7.AR.2.2	Modeling Using Equations or Inequalities		
MA.7.AR.3.1 MA.7.AR.3.2	Applying Ratios and Percents		
MA.7.AR.3.3	Unit Rates		
MA.7.AR.4.1	Understanding and Representing Proportions		
MA.7.AR.4.2	Finding Constant of Proportionality		
MA.7.AR.4.3	Significance of points on graphs of proportions		
MA.7.AR.4.4	Represent proportions by equations		
MA.7.GR.1.1	Area of Polygons		
MA.7.GR.1.2	Finding Area, Volume, & Surface Area		
MA.7.GR.1.3 MA.7.GR.1.4	Circles		
MA.7.GR.1.5	Scale models		
MA.7.GR.2.1 MA.7.GR.2.2	Surface Area of Cylinders		
MA.7.GR.2.3	Volume of Cylinders		

Standard	Lesson	Score	Date of Completion
BEST			
MA.7.DP.1.1	Context of Data Gathered		
MA.7.DP.1.1	Relating Data Distributions		
MA.7.DP.1.2	Mean, Median, and Mean Absolute Deviation		
MA.7.DP.1.2	Mean, Median, and Mode		
MA.7.DP.1.3	Sampling a Population		
MA.7.DP.1.3	Describing Multiple Samples		
MA.7.DP.1.4	Circle Graphs		
MA.7.DP.1.5	Graphical Representation of Data		
MA.7.DP.2.1	Sample Space of an Event		
MA.7.DP.2.2	Understanding Probability		
MA.7.DP.2.3	Predicting Using Probability		
MA.7.DP.2.4	Using Probability Models		
MA.7.DP.2.4	Probability Models from Observed Frequencies		

Made in United States
Orlando, FL
19 January 2024

42646459R00126